# Every Crushing Stroke

**The Book of Performance Kayaking**

**CRAB APPLE PUBLISHING**

## Acknowledgements:

This book has been more a compilation of ideas that I have
learned from many people. I owe many thanks to many people for all that they
have taught me both in my paddling career and in writing this book. I would
like to especially thank Bill Endicott, Sylvan Poberaj, Kent Ford, Larry
Norman, Chris Smith, Ken Redmond, Peter Kennedy-Lee, Peter Stekel, Bunni
Labadic, and so many others who have contributed to this project. Special
thanks also to Rick Achberger for the tremendous job he did in typesetting.

# TABLE OF CONTENTS

| | |
|---|---|
| **Introduction** | **5** |
| | |
| **The Olympic Revolution** | **6** |
| Biography | 6 |
| | |
| **Technique** | **23** |
| The Strokes | 23 |
| Forward Stroke | 23 |
| Turning the Boat | 27 |
| Forward Sweep | 28 |
| Back Sweep | 31 |
| Draws | 33 |
| Upstreams | 36 |
| Offsets | 51 |
| | |
| **Training Section** | **60** |
| Yearly Training Plan | 60 |
| Learning Technique | 61 |
| Strength Training | 64 |
| Lactic Training | 67 |
| Aerobic Training | 69 |
| The Yearly Training Plan | 71 |
| Making a Yearly Plan | 72 |
| Making Weekly Schedules | 75 |
| Race Prep: The Final Five Weeks | 77 |
| Race Day | 79 |
| | |
| **Section 5: Fifty Workouts** | **84** |
| Introduction | 84 |
| **Lactic Endurance** | **85** |
| 45"on 2:15" med | 85 |
| Shadow Loops | 85 |
| McLoops | 86 |
| 2' on 30" off | 86 |
| 2' on 1' off | 87 |
| 3' on 30" off | 87 |
| 3' on 1' off | 88 |
| 3'on 2' off | 88 |
| 3'on 6' med, Flatwater Distance | 89 |
| 5' on 1' off | 89 |
| Brute-Loops | 90 |
| Phase Change Loops | 90 |

| | |
|---|---|
| Pursuit-Loops | 91 |
| 10' on 2' med | 91 |
| 15' on 2' med | 92 |
| 20' on 2' med | 92 |
| 30' on | 93 |
| Distance | 93 |
| **Lactic** | **94** |
| 60's | 94 |
| 60's | 94 |
| Offset 60's | 95 |
| Fulls | 95 |
| Mock-race | 96 |
| Qualifier-finals Fulls | 96 |
| Course Change fulls | 97 |
| Pacing Fulls | 97 |
| **Lactic Tolerance** | **98** |
| 30" on, 30" off | 98 |
| 40" on 20" off | 98 |
| Berger loops | 99 |
| Short Rest Brokens | 99 |
| 1' on 20" off | 100 |
| 4' on 6' off | 100 |
| **Technique/Power** | **101** |
| 5 x 5's | 101 |
| Brokens | 101 |
| Impossible Moves | 102 |
| World Cup Shorts | 102 |
| Singles Shorts | 103 |
| Team Shorts | 103 |
| Consistency Loops | 104 |
| Funnel Sprints | 104 |
| Stroke Drills | 105 |
| Specific Technique | 105 |
| Teacher Shorts | 106 |
| Easy to Hard Shorts | 106 |
| Technique over Drops | 107 |
| Minimum Stroke Shorts | 107 |
| Single Run Shorts | 108 |
| Slow to Fast Shorts | 108 |
| Whitewater Moves Shorts | 109 |
| C-1 Shorts | 109 |

# Introduction

*"And confidence-Scott Shipley calls it necessary arrogance-is not just a mental state of mind but a result of having performed up to your personal expectations many times under race conditions"*
—Jon Lugbill, Five-time World Champion

I can still remember being 14 and seeing Five-time World Champions Jon Lugbill and Richard Fox paddle for the first time. It was so incredible to see such perfection, grace and precision as it approached me. It was equally incredible to watch them storm past and realize the power they put into each stroke and see the speed they took out of it. These two athletes, along with a select few others had taken the sport of whitewater slalom to a level it had never seen before. Until then racers had mostly scratched the surface of our sport, these elite few had reached deep inside our sport and begun to truly understand the deeply hidden secrets of whitewater slalom. These few great paddlers were the first to dominate a slalom course with every crushing stroke they took. This book unlocks the secrets of performing at that supreme level. It is a guide to the technique, training, and racing of today's elite slalom athletes. This is a blueprint for excellence that can take you, stroke by crushing stroke, from where you are now to the opening ceremonies of the next Olympiad.

This is a difficult sport to quantify. There are so many different ways to be a successful slalom athlete and, assuming they lead to success, one is not necessarily more correct than the next. This book is not meant to be a scientific formula for success at slalom. In fact, it is meant to be almost the opposite: it is a guide to how slalom athletes paddle and train today-the layman's book of slalom. In many instances the techniques and training are common to all slalom athletes. We all, for example, do three or more technique workouts a week in the spring; we all do them in roughly the same way. In other instances, such as warm-ups and race preparation, the experience will be so deeply personal that I don't even try and create a consensus. This is a book of how and why I trained and raced the way I did. In some cases the techniques described in this book are used by most top-level athletes, in other cases I have included my own training secrets.

Every Crushing Stroke starts from the very beginning. It is a guide for whitewater athletes and coaches of all levels. It breaks down every stroke to point out the fundamentals of good stroke technique. As you become proficient at the basics you can learn to tweak each and every stroke you take for the utmost in power, precision, and efficiency. This book also takes you through the basics of gate technique.

For every paddler there is a progression. Starting with the essential techniques of slalom, it teaches the paddler where they must place the boat, how and where to turn the boat, and other basic racing techniques that make up the backbone of racing. Each skill also has a section for advanced and elite athletes. You can use these technical refinements as a progression for your own development in this sport. There is the advanced level. For those who are proficient at standard technique this is a refined method. This second, more difficult level, takes the racer another step towards the perfect run. This refined technique puts the paddlers on the same path as the World_s greatest by teaching them the same lines that the world's greatest use. The third and final level takes good paddlers and makes them into world-class athletes, able to match any paddler anywhere. These are the techniques and lines that National team coaches and World Champion athletes use to win races.

The second section of Every Crushing Stroke contains the nuts and bolts of training, the how-to_s of physical training for slalom as well as a guide to putting together your year's training plan. This section starts out by teaching you the fundamentals of physical training for slalom. It sets the objectives and describes the protocol for doing effective physical and technical training for slalom. This section will also take you through your year's training and describe in detail how to mesh all your workouts into a yearly training plan. You will find this guide takes you from your first stroke of fall training right through the last stroke of your most important race.

The final section of this book is a guide to almost every workout you'll need to know for effective slalom training. Fifty different workouts are described in detail. Athletes and coaches will be able to use this section as a guide to make their training focused and interesting. This guide will help athletes and coaches choose the right workout at the right pace for the right time of the year.

**SCOTT SHIPLEY
1996 OLYMPICS**
The author, 3 time World Cup Champion Scott Shipley making his third Olympic Team. Photo by Chris Smith.

# The Olympic Revolution

*"Before you claim that you are 'committed to slalom' I want you to picture what went in to your last breakfast of ham and eggs. The chicken was merely involved in creating that breakfast, the pig...the pig was committed"*
-Lecky Haller, Two-time Olympian

## Getting Started

It's hard to explain in today's slalom terms, to people who know slalom as an Olympic sport, what our sport was like only ten years ago. We who were there are now "old-school"–we were kayakers before people knew what kayakers were. So much about our sport changed when we became an Olympic event. To be a full-time kayaker ten years ago put you one rung above a longhaired skateboarding teenager on the scale of social grace. Times have changed. We are no longer the futureless renegade drop-outs, Kayak-parents no longer describe their sons and daughters as people who are "Trying to find themselves" or "Taking a break from their goals". No, now we are Olympians. Put any eight to twenty-nine year old in a kayak and he's no longer learning to kayak, he's an "Olympic Hopeful." Gone are the days when we stood in the shadow of more respectable sports. Kayakers now adorn the pages of Sports Illustrated and are broadcast daily into our homes in an attempt to sell more cars and computers. We have yet to become a "rich" sport yet we are wealthy beyond the wildest dreams of our recent predecessors—an evolution that has meant more coaching, more support, and more sponsorship. The Olympic family has welcomed us into their fold, and in so doing has forever changed the face of slalom in America.

In 1980 our sport was different. Sport Utility Vehicles had not yet replaced the rusted V.W. vans and ratty old station wagons that had formerly transported our sport. Trips to Europe were frequently paid for with re-allocated student loans or odd jobs worked in D.C. neighborhoods. I can remember Jed Prentice, Junior World C-1 champion, driving to a four-day training camp with a jar of peanut butter, a jar of jelly, three cans of powdered carbo-drink, and some vitamin supplements. We were on borrowed time because we had neither the money nor the credibility to put aside our lives for very long. To commit yourself to a year of full-time training in our sport was to betray any hopes your family and friends had that you'd become a success at life. I hear people talk about being committed kayaking now and think of them as bungee jumpers leaping off of a bridge while strapped to rubber bands carefully calibrated to cushion their landings. Whether they make it or not, they are golden children to their families and friends. Such a grand objective! The champions of yesteryear were the base-jumpers who made a leap of faith before they unfurled their chutes with their talent and dedication; there were no soft landings for the weak-hearted in that day. Make or miss the team and you were still likely to hit rock bottom. We were the black sheep; we were the ones who had put aside our goals to go paddling.

In 1980 names like Jon Lugbill and David and Cathy Hearn raced across our sport like wildfire. America had won medals! Even before I knew I was missing a hero in this sport we had made to order ones flashing across our newly invented VCRs. Lugbill was the consummate champion—aggressive and bold all the way to the finish, Davey the technician—precise and calculating. In Cathy we saw our first look at an uber-woman who would sit at the peak of our sport for a generation. We watched these paddlers in the one spotlight available at the time, in a movie called "Fast and Clean." It was an all at once thriller, documentary and infomercial for the sport of kayaking and the deeds of these great paddlers. I grew up watching and re-watching that film and dreaming of attaining or surpassing their deeds. Not once in all that time did I crave the riches of a pro athlete or the recognition of an Olympian. I wanted to be like my heroes. I wanted to drive to Jonquiere in my green Cathy Hearn style Pinto and I wanted to launch myself out of the starting gate like Austrian Norbert Sattler. I wanted to be the fastest kayaker in the World.

My father had learned to paddle from his father—presumably his father could say the same thing about my great-grandfather. There seems to be a Shipley way to learn to paddle, passed on from generation to generation and unchanged by any improvements in

Photo by Ken Redmond.

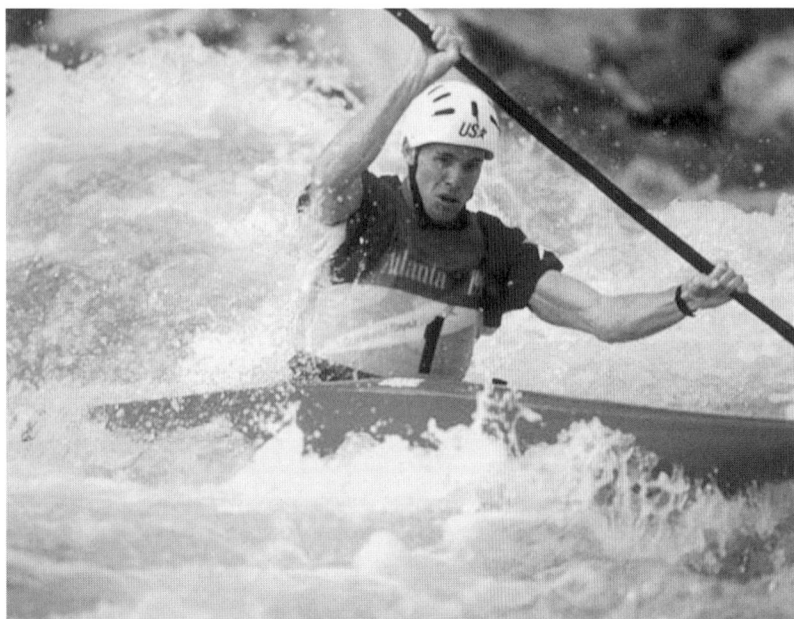

technology. I took my first strokes in the same aluminum canoe that my father had paddled with his father. We used ancient paddles carved from a single piece of wood and sewed our own paddling gear. Our paddle jackets were last year's windbreakers with neoprene cuffs sewed on the arms. Our early spraydecks were sewn by hand using the same patterns my grandmother had created for some of the first fiberglass boats ever to be paddled in this country.

River running, in my father's time, was done with local clubs. It is an affiliation you still see in Europe although it has become rare in the U.S. This meant that my earliest experiences in paddling were far from the nearest gate course. Instead we spent our weekends exploring different northwest rivers in our big Canadian-style canoe. My father craved adventure in the truest and purest form, which had the side effect of making these weekend excursions wet, cold, and miserable. He believed in roughing it and learning the old way and our weekend excursions were no exception. We shivered through weekend after weekend in our leaky age-old tent. Our homemade gear steamed in a ring around a blazing fire while we feasted on the food my father never learned how to cook.

We ran all these rivers as a family team in our great canoe. My Dad was in the back and either my brother or I in the front, the remainder in the middle. We took turns reading the rivers and deciding which route the family would take down the next set of rapids. Both my brother and I argued over who would sit in the bow and which eddies we would catch or miss. As you can imagine it wasn't long before we outgrew this arrangement and needed another boat to keep us separated.

Our first kayak was a monstrous boat, still the biggest kayak I've ever owned, and this became our sidecar. As it turned out this couldn't have been a better arrangement. My brother and I, who normally argued and fought over everything, would race to be the opposite in this case. Paul desperately wanted to paddle canoe with my dad and I, more desperately than anything, wanted to be in that kayak.

Our training situation was a bit awkward at the time. We grew up by the water on the shores of Puget Sound and had the scope of the Pacific Ocean at our disposal. This meant we could paddle as much as we wanted to. Unfortunately, the Pacific, even in the narrowest of its local inlets, was too wide for gate wires and we were limited to a single gate hung from a local pier. Our closest training course was more than an hour's drive away. Instead we would snake in and out of the different piers, do sprints from here to there and back again, fill the boats with water and pretend we could do the same monstrous pivots that we had heard Lugbill and Hearn were doing. It was the sort of training site that would either become completely stifling, or, as was later to be the case, a spawning ground for innovation.

Essentially our training was one of two things. Either we were sprinting around the sound in some form or another, or else we were running rivers. River running was the thing we did that probably had the most effect on our abilities later. My dad was big on

finding adventures so we were constantly in search of new experiences. We ran all sorts of rivers, everything from huge big water to tiny tributaries. We'd go to the ocean and surf waves or we'd lower ourselves down seventy feet of rope on muddy cliffs so that we could run Pilchuck creek in flood. Every weekend was a new adventure often in a new place. In today's slalom world future Olympians are weaned on flatwater courses and coached gate technique workouts. My brother Paul and I cut our teeth two hundred feet deep in the snowy Green River gorge surfing four foot curling waves while we shivered in our wool underwear and homemade jackets.

Although we spent most of our time running rivers, my brother and I were entranced with slalom racing. My father had raced for the U.S. National team in the sixties and we begged him to take us to races. This was not an easy task in the Northwest at the time. Our sport had a small following and a limited number of races every year. The entire area boasted only a single permanent flatwater training site. In spite of our lack of slalom courses we thought of ourselves as nothing less than slalom racers. For fifteen years not a single race happened within a three state radius of our home without the Shipleys being there. I had been involved in many sports before we began paddling but quit those teams rather than waste more time on an endeavor that got in the way of slalom. Both my brother and I latched on to paddling with fervor from the first strokes we took. Neither one of us ever stopped to decide if we wanted to dedicate ourselves to this sport; it was something we just knew from the start.

We had a fairly active group of slalom athletes in our area at the time. Five to ten of us would meet Wednesday nights in Seattle for slalom workouts on the Northwest's lone flatwater slalom course. Occasionally we would set up a moving water course on the Cedar river and make the hour and a half trek to train there twice a week. We had no coach at the time but I can rattle off a long list of people who, in

**SCOTT TRAINING AS A KID**
Scott Shipley racing as a Junior
Photo by Sue Shipley.

the absence of a trainer, took the place of a coach for us. The entire training group fed each other training tips and times or else organized and hosted workouts and races. We were one of the most unified training groups I've ever been a part of despite the fact so few of us had any intention of taking our pursuit of the sport out of the Northwest.

Much of my early paddling technique came from my father, but I really started to make jumps in my paddling when a local racer, John Day, began working with me during our Wednesday night gate sessions. John was, at the time, one of the top ten paddlers in the United States. He had a long slow stroke rate and was masterful at gliding through gates and using whitewater to make moves easier—I adopted all of these attributes and made them my own. In the Northwest John, along with his brother Mike—who was often back east racing—were the top of the heap. When they began a run all of us would rush down the course to see as much of their paddling as possible.

Photo by Ken Redmond.

They were the best of their time. Since they traveled the world to bigger paddling events they were also our only source of new techniques and equipment.

When I was little I would target people in my training. At the end of each season I would pick someone I wanted to better by the next year and then spend the winter training to beat him. At first, this meant beating the local masters champion, then the fastest lady in our club until eventually I was chasing my mentors themselves. I grew up with an overwhelming desire to compete, to be faster, to beat people. Every workout and every race I was focused on attack, attack, attack. If I was slower than my target, I would dig deeper to paddle better and faster on my next effort. The great lesson I took from these early years was the respect we all shared despite how competitive these workouts and races were. At the tick of a watch we were desperately racing to beat our training partners yet moments later, when the watch was off, we would help each other. We were teammates in the truest sense.

## Racing

Today, juniors come from training centers. The best of these juniors come from organized programs with coaches and training partners. In my time it was different. Our country had a smattering of juniors training largely on their own around the country. The first time I raced another junior from America was after a five-day road trip across America. We were a hodge-podge of people from across the states. For most of us the Junior Nationals was the one chance we had to see each other compete for the entire year. Was I a dark horse? We all were dark horses. I was twelve the first year I competed there and only a year or two younger than most of the serious competitors. We came through as a pack of talented cadets who could already best the country's top juniors.

There was little back then in the way of a junior racing circuit. Often we would all meet at a Junior training camp for a week or so before the Nationals to train together. Then we would each race at the Junior Nationals and either win or else return home to train up for the following year's race. On my first try I finished a respectable fourth. By my third shot at Nationals I had worked my way up to second—the last time I would ever leave this race without a National title.

There were some real benefits to being a junior in a sport that didn't have any funding. Top racers were desperately in need of money and would gladly hire themselves out as coaches for a week here or a week there. These became a yearly destination for my brother and I. There wasn't much money in the sport at the time, neither for the top athletes nor the families who supported these athletes. My parents were no different and could only really afford to send Paul and I across the country once a year. We'd squeeze the rock to get as much from these trips as possible. Paul and I would arrange to take part in one of these camps before bumming a ride to the Nationals from there. We'd be coached by the likes of Jon Lugbill, Mike McCormick, and Richard Weiss. They were the best of their time and I was all at once in awe of knowing them as well as determined to learn to match their skills.

I sometimes think that the US should continue those camps as they were. These were the precursors to New England's Adventure Quest and the NRC junior camps. I think they were some of the best learning experiences of my developing years. Often the Nationals would be a part of a series of races. Organizers like Peter Kennedy would arrange and help coach the camps such that we could spend three weeks racing in the Mid-America Series while attending training camps between each race. It was the kind of made-to-order perfect training that kids have very little access too. Like so many things these camps fell victim to our Olympic initiation. Big sponsors took over the series and made it an elite-level professional series. The junior camps just faded away.

The eighties were the heyday of the U.S. C-1s and Britain's Richard Fox. It seems now like the world of paddling put aside its collective thinking caps to mimic these great paddlers. Rather than testing new techniques or designing new boats we simply followed the lead of these elite few. Any jewel of knowledge that came from these training camps started with "Lugbill says..." or "Fox did it like...". This attitude was especially pervasive in the U.S. where we were so proud of the results our canoes were producing. Our junior training camps focused on learning to paddle like these C-1s by mimicking their flashy pivoting upstreams and aggressive attacking style. New techniques came down from the top; they were innovated by Lugbill and Hearn, refined by their now famous technician/coach Bill Endicott and then became the gospel we preached to each other.

Winning the Nationals became an obsession for me. With each loss I would rededicate myself to success in the coming year. Often, especially at first, an entire year of waiting for my next shot seemed like an unending eternity. I would later find that it was just enough time to get ready. My training at home would become stricter and more regimented each year. At first it was my goal to ensure I paddled every day during the week; then I began to focus on improving the quality and duration of these efforts. No longer was it good enough to just be paddling every day. I began to focus on making each workout count, to make a real improvement each time I got on the water. I could feel myself getting better and better each year, but I could also see my competitors doing the same thing. Despite my improvements I was disappointed to find that three years of training had only brought me half the way I needed to go to win the Junior Nationals.

## The Junior Circuit

Two big things happened in 1986 that changed the way things were heading. My brother Paul got his driver's license and we discovered the Canadian National team training site in Chilliwack, British Columbia—about four hours from our house. Chilliwack is an end-of-the-road town in one of the rainiest parts of the entire Northwest. Make no mistake about this place, it is cold, constantly cloudy, and the winter days are barely long enough to allow two workouts. Canadian team member Larry Norman summed up the situation best when he said; "The weather here is easy to predict, if you can see the mountains it's going to rain, if you can't see the mountains...it is raining".

It was a dark, dreary, and depressing place to train. If the clouds do clear you can see that the river cuts through the harsh Canadian wilderness. The sharp snow-covered crags of the Canadian Coastal range surround the river. More often than not we awoke to find those mountains cloaked in a heavy layer of clouds that left the valley dark and shaded. Our view would reach only a few hundred feet up the valley walls and merely revealed that the snow line was closer that morning than we had hoped. Instead of awakening to a stunning vista of our mountainous surroundings we were often as not surrounded in mist and rain and leaves rotting beneath a thin layer of snow

This was our gymnasium, nothing less and nothing more. We lacked any sort of conventional clubhouse or training center. We changed our clothes in the dirt beside our cars and we trained in the stadium that God gave us.

What a stadium it was though, there are few places in the world that can compare to the training site in which we paddled daily on the Chilliwack river. The rapid is a powerful class three to four rapid that cuts through the rugged Canadian wilderness. The river there is about 30 meters wide and littered with obstacles leaving an almost infinite number of gate combinations. The site also has three big areas of drop separated by three separate easier sections that can be easily attained by training athletes. As athletes, this gave us three completely separate training basins in which to train. In short, it is everything you could hope for in a natural training site. Day after day and week after week we could train in what was almost—excepting the cold and wet— ideal conditions. Our full-lengths were the equal of most World Cup courses and everything from short courses to long endurance could be done in the best of settings.

Chilliwack became a weekly destination for Paul and I and the world we paddled in began to change radically. Although I missed paddling with our old club we almost instantly switched from being active club members to being fanatical racers. The group we now paddled with were of a similar mind: train better, train smarter, and get faster. Since no one ever really wanted to live in Chilliwack our training group was mostly made up of people like us. We had homes in Seattle, Bellingham or Vancouver and we commuted to Chilliwack for the weekend's workouts. Each Saturday morning we would rally by the river at 9:00 to set a full-length course.

For the first time Paul and I had access to a full-length slalom course, like-minded training partners, and a long-term coaching relationship. To say we had a coach is true, but not in the terms people think of today. This was still the time before there were paid coaches in North America. Coaches like Bill Endicott and my coach, Eric Munshaw, were few and far between. Like the rest of us they were unpaid in any way. These people volunteered their time, paid their own expenses, and often made as many or more sacrifices than their athletes.

With 20/20 hindsight people must assume that I was the little starling favored by coaches and clubs alike as I was growing up. This was never the case. Early on I was an awkward youth and there was barely enough coaching available for even the World Class athletes in our country. Still, Eric managed the time to work with some of us on a sporadic basis. On average I would say I had two coached workouts a month from Eric and there were two big ways that he affected my paddling:

The first was that Eric was constantly holding training camps where we would work together as a group. In these camps he would hold nightly sessions where he lectured us on race-preparation, visualization, making training plans and keeping training logs. I soaked up his lessons like a sponge. He was the first one to put ideas into my head about organizing our training, making a race plan for every run—in both training and race situations, and learning to focus my technique sessions so that I improved at an astounding rate.

Suddenly my training was no longer a slap-shot collection of randomly chosen workouts. Things that I take for granted now, like our long endurance workouts in the fall and our lactic training in the spring were suddenly revealed to me. Where I had once been wandering around in the dark doing whichever workout seemed appropriate I now focused my efforts. I felt I was now learning to aim my training directly along the shortest path to World Championship medals—I had begun to train efficiently.

Knowing how to train in a kayak and knowing how to paddle a kayak are entirely different things. In America, the 80's were the era of the American C-1s and we all marched to the tune of their success. Despite Fox's many World Championship wins, the fittest of American kayaks spent their technique sessions learning the windshield-wiper pivots and sit-and-spin style that our canoes were using to dominate the Europeans. Any coach worth his salt in America preached their tune and any paddler hoping for success fell in line to follow their beat. In many ways we Americans were like so many sheep following a single shepherd*.

Whether it was because he was isolated from the roar of their success or because he saw their success for what it was—domination of the canoe class— Eric shunned the American's paddling. To say Eric taught me the secrets of great kayakers would be an exaggeration. He didn't know their secrets any more than the rest of us. The truth is that no one in North America knew them at the time, no one. What Eric taught us was that paddling like a C-1 wasn't going to beat the likes of Richard Fox. We had to find a better way. We had to teach ourselves to paddle kayaks like kayaks. The second thing Eric taught us was to discover these things for ourselves.

On the water, which is to say after we had prepared for our workouts, Eric focused on two things. The first of these was that I paddle from the bow and forgo the large pivots and sit-back style of my American compatriots. "Push the bow Scotty," he'd say, "Get off the stern and push your knees where you want the boat to go." I was young and like all youngsters I preferred my newly mastered big pivots and flashy spins. Eric favored a more toned down— keep the boat running approach to paddling. He would push us to practice doing moves off the bow. We would practice banking turns and edge control to work on keeping the boat moving through our turns.

The other thing he brought to our on the water workouts was a focus to our training. We would isolate just the thing we wanted to work on. It is common in today's world to focus on certain gate moves.

These are often very complicated gate moves and paddlers will isolate this move until they have mastered it. We did more than that; we isolated every part of our training. We would just sprint down through a rapid to focus on our paddling in whitewater, or we would pick a large, river-wide wave and practice the fastest way to cross that wave—without any gates! We did stroke drills, short courses with our eyes closed and a hundred different exercises designed to isolate a hundred different skills. Everything that was a part of our racing was isolated, broken down, and then put back together in its perfect form.

I look back now at how little we knew and wonder that we ever came as far as we did. We became the masters of bumbling our way to success. I can remember a particular workout where we were working on phase changes—the ability to change our pace in a race run. The idea goes something like this: If you are sprinting as fast as you can downstream against a competitor and you go five miles an hour while your competitor goes four miles an hour you will be only twenty percent faster than your competition. To put this in a real context lets say you sprint out of the starting gate and arrive at the first gate eight seconds later. When you get there you will have gained two seconds—at a grave expense of energy—on your competitors.

Now let's say further down the river you are doing an upstream in the current so that you must paddle against a three mile per hour current. Again you sprint at five miles an hour and your competitor at four. Now you are going twice the speed of your competitor! In the two seconds it takes you to do this gate you gain the same two seconds on your competition. We were looking for those two easy seconds.

We came up with this theory at one point and decided to practice doing all our upstreams at a sprint. For our training we put together a forty-five second course with three or four upstreams and did runs where we emphasized the slow and the fast. As we paddled between the upstreams we cruised and let the boat glide. Then as we approached the upstreams we'd pour on the gas and sprint into and out of the gate with hopes of gaining a second on our competitors. Was the workout a success? Not even close, not a single one of us could consistently do a good turn after sprinting into the upstream. Our pacing was off, our accuracy was horrendous and all of us constantly hit the poles. However we knew the theory was good and we hammered away at the details for weeks. What eventually came of the workouts is now standard technique that any beginning junior could tell you: Approach your upstreams with control, precision, and preparation—exit them with crushingly powerful strokes. Come in precisely and leave powerfully.

To truly understand the sort of training we were doing in those days I think it is important to put the sum of my training as a junior in context. I trained on gateless flatwater five days out of seven; I traveled four hours to Canada every weekend to train with the Canadian team there. I was coached for maybe two

---

*It should be noted that Endicott and many of our top C-1s were strongly influenced by Fox's style. However, in speaking with many of the kayaks of that era all have remarked that the D.C. C-1s had the largest influence on their technique.

weeks during the summer and a weekend or two a month throughout the winter. My training partners were an incredibly keen group of C-1s and women kayakers and the nearest competitive K-1 junior lived 3,000 miles from my house. Most athletes today would look at this situation as primitive and substandard. By today's standards I had no training site, no coaching, and no competitors. However, the situation had the advantage of forcing me to find alternative methods of training—many of which shaped the way I paddled for the rest of my career.

They say necessity is the father of invention and this could not have been truer than it was for my training in those days. I had a flatwater lake but was competing every weekend against the C-1s and K-1ws that were training full-time on whitewater gates. I took Eric's lessons to heart and found workouts on flatwater that isolated every part of a slalom run on whitewater. I did sprints that went sideways to work on my rotation and sprints with five starts and five stops to work on my acceleration. I invented these and a million other drills to make up for the time I was missing in gates.

I became the master of self-evaluation. Each weekend was a test that I invariably failed for some reason or another. If I felt I was slower because of bad offsets one weekend I'd hang my single gate and work on offsets every day that week until I had become perfect at offsets. The next week I might have trouble with my full-spins and do the same. It was a fantastic system of training because it became a weekly cycle of evaluation and improvement. Where my competitors were training rhythmically for the year only to test themselves at the next big event I was, on a weekly basis, re-evaluating my performance and finding ways to improve it. I inch-wormed my way to the top by constantly raising the level of my weakest points. Ladies World Champion Lynn Simpson told me once that she used to work the same way, focusing on her weak elements until they became her strong elements. This is a parallel in our training that I found fascinating. I've since concluded that it is this ability to recognize your weaknesses that makes great champions. A little self-criticism can go a long way in this sport.

## The Junior Worlds

I had not been able to race the Junior Worlds in 1986 because it would have been too expensive to send both Paul and I to Europe in the same year. Paul was older and this was his only shot at that race. He finished a respectable thirteenth. Like all of our American C-1s he was extremely quick—fast enough for third—but had fallen victim to gate penalties on the day of the race. I had been crushed to have been left behind while all of my rivals raced Europeans that summer. I was in agony all summer knowing that I was spinning my wheels in my hometown of Poulsbo while people I could beat were racing in Germany and Austria. The idea that finances had kept me off a team I deserved to be on burned in the back of my head as I stormed through my workouts that summer.

The end result of being left home was that the US kayaks came home to the Junior Nationals confident of their abilities while I left Poulsbo hungry for that title. In fact, our team had been so confident that year that as I paddled into the starting gate a team boat asked for an extra minute so he wouldn't "catch me"! I couldn't believe my ears! An extra minute is reserved solely for the whitewater handicapped—those who can't manage to be swept downriver at an equitable enough pace to avoid being caught. My resolve to dominate that race was redoubled right there in the starting gate. I have won a few National titles in my life, but none were quite so satisfying as the first one, the title I won with an extra minute gap behind me.

An entire summer of wishing I was in Europe almost made that first National Championship a moot point. Before I ever took a single stroke in that race I was already dreaming of bigger things. The Junior Worlds had become the next target on my "hit list".

Winning the Junior Worlds was a whole different class of race however. Try to think of it this way: Pick any sport you like and imagine the best guy at your high school, then imagine the best guy in your region, then the best guy in your state. Take it a step further and imagine the best of the state champions: the National champion. The Junior Worlds is the collection of these elite athletes from around the world. The Junior World Champion is the best of these best. I was fifteen when I won my first National title, that same night I focused my sights on this new achievement. I would be Junior World Champion.

I have always had an overabundance of confidence. Growing up I was cocky beyond what most people can even imagine. I had come to my first National Championships secure in the knowledge that I would leave a champion, despite being 12 years old. In fact, I'm almost embarrassed to admit that I was sure I would win the open class! This was an attribute that a U.S. team coach first identified as "Necessary Arrogance". This was supreme confidence and it was a mindset that had its advantages. While others would write off early races as being a learning experience I would compete with a singular frame of mind. When I leave the starting gate I'm not out to learn anything. Since my first start in my first race I have always left the starting gate with a single objective—I want to beat everybody!

Once I set my goal of being the best in the world I was stunned to find that no one but myself believed I could actually win that title! The Slovenians had finished first, second and fourth in the previous Junior Worlds and the idea that they, along with the other Europeans, were unbeatable had become entrenched in our Junior program. At this point no American men's kayaker had ever stood on an awards platform at a World Championship and many had come to believe that the Europeans were invincible. Some naysayers actually laughed when I told them I wanted to win this race. One of my own team coaches actually told me I couldn't win!

The Junior Worlds are a tough race to forecast. The race only takes place every second year. By the time the next Junior Worlds would come around the field would change almost entirely. Quite often the fastest boats at one Junior Worlds would outgrow their positions before the next. Despite the rotating team roster the Europeans had consistently good results. These results came from extremely well run junior programs. Year after year they would create fast juniors because they had great coaches, great facilities, and great competition. On a team level this was an intimidating prospect on a personal level it meant very little. As I said before, I was never lacking in self-confidence. I reasoned that there was the same amount of training time in a day over there as we had in America.

At the age of 16 I finally managed to qualify for the National Junior team. In a stroke of luck I also made the senior team at those same selections. This allowed me to compete at the Pre-World Championships on the Savage River in Maryland—an event that served as valuable preparation for the Junior Worlds.

Photo by Ken Redmond

The Savage Worlds was a difficult race for the Europeans. It was held only a few hours from the U.S.'s major training center in Washington D.C. but a long plane ride from any of their home courses. To make things even more difficult there was a very limited supply of water for practice time on the course. There were only three time slots a day to be divided up amongst all the competitors—leaving many desperate for every bit of water time available. The course was packed with athletes, which made training difficult at the best of times. In spite of the crowds I remember being stunned to see Britain's Richard Fox charge through the pack with little or no resistance. The crowds of paddlers seemed to part like the Red Sea in order to allow the champion through.

My experience was just the opposite. I was used to the sparsely populated rivers of the Northwest. I would politely allow this paddler or that to go ahead as I tried to train among the masses. Everyone ran me over, I managed one or two runs a workout and

once was run over by a Czeck C-2 team while walking up the trail! I mentioned my frustrations to a fellow teammate who was also racing in her first International race. I remember clearly her response; "Well, remember you're here for the same reason I am: to have fun and get some experience. Don't lose track of that". I almost fell off my chair listening to her! I wasn't here for experience; I was here to win this race. After two days of being pushed around I vowed to play hardball. I became a heat-seeking missile. I cut off any and everyone and would charge after those who did the same to me. Every run became one big team run in combination with whoever happened to be in my way. I let nothing and nobody stop my workouts

I had learned my lesson well and brought those experiences to the Junior Worlds. I had concluded that there were too many extras that go along with these big races and most of them were just a big hassle for those who were there to win. I avoided parades, team dinners and team meetings. I used only the coaching staff that proved most helpful and avoided those who seemed to be wasting my time. I trained here as I had trained in my final few workouts at the Pre-Worlds, by charging though an overcrowded field of competitors with a take-no-prisoners attitude. An attitude that shocked these juniors the way it had shocked me just one month beforehand. In short, I turned my back on many of the opportunities surrounding this event and raced my own race instead.

In many ways this race was very intimidating. For the first time in my life I was up against a large pack of people that were the same speed I was. We were assigned "training slots" by country and given specific times in which we were allowed to train at the race site itself. I would spend hours with my teammates every day watching the other countries training. I was in awe of all the talented kids from across Europe. True to form the Slovenians fielded three strong boats once again, as did almost every other European country. I counted three strong Brits, three strong Germans, three strong French and many others. There were more than a hundred kayaks in the Men's class alone!

My biggest concern while traveling over to Europe had been the course itself. I knew my strengths and weaknesses and hoped that this course would play into them. If the race was set on difficult whitewater, much like the rivers I was used to training on, I reasoned I would be in good shape, if it were set on an easier rapid I felt I would most likely fall victim to the Europeans, who I felt had better gate skills. I remember driving up to the course and being so disappointed at what I saw. The river was virtually a creek with what seemed like very easy whitewater.

What I couldn't see from my elevated vantage point was that this indeed was big water. I was looking down on a steep, tight creek with sharp rocks and vicious holes. This was intimidating whitewater. On our first run through I was flipped end for end and two of my teammates swam. I was ecstatic! This was exactly the sort of water I'd been hoping for and the course turned out to be a real advantage for me. On the whole the water was fast, pushy, and intimidating.

The race was seeded by dividing the results into thirds—if your boat finished in the first third at the previous Worlds then they would start in the first third at these championships. The country order was decided by draw. This left our entire team, all three boats, in the worst third of the race! I finished my first run more than an hour and a half before the entire field was posted. I was young then and felt like I should be put at the end of the pack with the better boats but in the end I think the seed worked to our advantage. I led that first run by a full fourteen seconds! This was a huge lead. Since we had started so early nobody had bothered to watch my team-mates and I do our runs. We weren't on anyone's video or anyone's splits yet I was able to watch virtually every one of my top competitors do their runs.

My second run was within a couple seconds of my first but the Europeans had begun to catch up. The ninety minutes between the finish of my second run and the finish of the race seemed like an eternity. My teammate Brad Nelson had finished his second run in second place although his position proved much more precarious and he started to drop as the results from the top boats came in. In the end I had my title and Brad finished in sixth place. Both of us had made vast improvements on our country's previous best of thirty-sixth place at these championships. For the first time America was making waves in the men's kayak class.

## Coming of Age

In 1989 our sport came of age in America. These were the glory days of U.S. slalom. It was the year we hosted a World Championship on the Savage river in Maryland and then categorically dominated the event. This was the first time ever we had attracted a large crowd and then captivated them with this sport. The banks of the Savage River played host to thirty thousand people and not one of them, myself included, could bear to sit as Jon Lugbilll charged by on his way to a twelve-second victory! It was stunning! Never before or since have I seen anyone attack a race run like that. It was inspiring and breathtaking at the same time. It was truly stunning to watch one of the greatest runs of all time.

Perhaps my most vivid memory from that event was the team run. In the starting gate Jon Lugbilll lined up behind Jed Prentice and Davey Hearn. Jon had won this event, Davey was second and Jed had finished in fourth, milliseconds out of a medal. Even before this race Jon and Davey had become demigods in our sport. Over a ten-year period they were virtually unbeaten and Jed, the 1986 Junior World Champion, was cast as their successor. What we knew at the time was that the prowess of these paddlers was of mythical proportions. What none of us could possibly know yet was that this was their swan song. Within two years the Europeans would catch our canoes and they would no longer dominate this field as they had for the past ten years. That was in the time to come, this was 1989 and it was beyond

belief that they could lose—for now the river was theirs. For this team run they had decided to send Jon first. For 10 years Jon and Davey had led a third boat to the Gold Medal podium in this event The expectation was that this year would be no different.

The Savage river sits in the heart of the Blue Ridge mountains, so named for the thick low mist that often coats its valleys. That mist was especially heavy on the Savage that day and the entire race had been plagued by a thick fog low to the river. The fog was so thick that at first we saw nothing. This was a two hundred second long course and all we could sense were the cheers of the crowd as the gang drew steadily nearer. Those cheers became a roar around us even as we squinted into the fog for any sign.

My most acute memory of that great day was a fist. The first thing to break the low-lying fog was Jon's fist. It was his top hand protruding above the mist and it hammered angrily into and out of the fog with each pounding stroke. Even before we could make

**CATHY HEARN**
One of America's greatest. Cathy Hearn was a bronze medallist in 1989 ten years after she won her first World Championship. Photo by Chris Smith.

out the rest of their bodies we could make out the three ghost-like fists of their top hands as they pumped furiously through the mist. This was a three-man team on a Lugbill-like charge down the course! Jon, Davey, and Jed each indistinguishable from the next, each of them champions in their own right. Finally the three of them surged out of the fog on a full speed sprint, deftly wove through the three or four gates within view, and then disappeared into the fog on their way down the course. With their passing so too passed the peak of their era. They belonged to another time; they were champions of the old school. With the finish of that day's race began a new era. No longer were we concerned with World Championship medals, all eyes focused now on Barcelona and its Olympic Games. We had only three years until the opening ceremonies.

For the U.S. team, 1989 was a tremendously successful year. For me it was my biggest failure. 1989 was my last year as a junior but I had wanted more than anything to race as an adult in those World Championships. It was bitterly disappointing to finish tenth in those selection races after having made the team the year before. Since I had won the Junior Worlds people had begun to speak to me as if it were now my destiny to race in the 1992 Olympics. All of the kids in my age group thought the same way. For some reason we had all assumed that our great team of 1989 would step aside and make way for the next generation. Our kayaks had been very successful at those Savage Worlds and I realized it was insane to believe they wouldn't fight tooth and nail for an Olympic berth. To be an Olympian in 1992 meant I had just three years to beat every American kayak, to be an Olympic Champion would likely take more than that.

On the other hand those Worlds inspired me. My arrogance had got the best of me once again and I focused my sights on Olympic Gold. I launched myself into my training like I never had before. For once I wasn't alone in this. My once remote training site in Canada became a Mecca for the top kayaks on the continent. Rich Weiss and Brian Brown from the U.S. moved there. Top Canadian performers David Ford and Patrice Gagnon also became residents. Mostly by coincidence we had become the greatest collection of North American kayaks ever put together. We trained in two separate groups for the bulk of our workouts, the Canadians in one group and us Americans in the other, but got together two or three times a week for our competitive workouts.

For ten years now American kayaks had been trying to match the dominating performances of our canoes. Many Americans paddled boats of similar design to the canoes, they trained the same way the canoes did, and they fashioned their technique off of the tight pivots our C-1s were making. This was a frustrating time for our kayaks. Many people spent their entire careers doing fourteen workouts a week and never knowing why it was that they couldn't catch the Europeans. By 1990 we were desperate to try something new and hired French coach Jean-Michele Prono to show us exactly what it was the

Europeans were doing that made them so successful.

Jean-Michele stressed a more subtle style than even what I had been practicing. He stressed preparation in almost every move. Where we had been trying to turn right in the gates we were now trying to turn above and through the gate while still keeping the speed on the boat. He taught us to use a bow-rudder to carry a turn instead of the blockier sharp turns we were doing on our heavy draws. Most importantly he stressed using our shoulders to lead and control our turns. We began to work on pocketing our upstreams with turns that would rocket us back into the current, our offsets were no longer random scrambles but controlled curves where again each gate seemed to launch us into the next. For some of us this camp was an epiphany. I had realized by this point that even my best was not as good as Richard Fox and that something had to change. I felt like Jean-Michele had finally supplied us with the know-how we needed to catch the Europeans. For others Jean-Michele's coaching was more difficult to accept.

For most Americans the Frenchman's coaching was a radical departure from the norm. As Americans, we had paddled one way for so many years that it was hard for many to accept that there was a better way. This was especially true for our canoes and women who had had so much success with the American style. There was a lot of resistance to these new ideas, especially in the East where it represented a smack in the face to our entrenched system. Once again my isolation proved to be my biggest advantage. While we were at the camp with Jean-Michele everyone was excited about his ideas. It was only after I went back to Chilliwack that many of the East Coast boaters came to doubt them. By that point I, and my west-coast training partners, were three thousand miles away and desperately trying to master Jean-Michelle's techniques.

These were stressful times for U.S. kayaks. In addition to our frustrations with our performances internationally there were added stresses at home. Worries about qualifying for the U.S. team were constantly weighing down my mind. While none of the US boats had reached a level where they were competitive with the best in the World there were many of us who were very competitive with each other. Every day, every workout and every run I worried that I was not fast enough to qualify for the U.S. team. The stress was a constant factor in the back of my mind. Some days I would be unbeatable in training and would glow for the rest of the day with the satisfaction of my performance. Other days I would make mistake after mistake and literally scream out loud with my frustrations.

Ironically it was out of fear of my competitors that I became motivated to master Jean-Michele's ideas. Our East coast competitors were able to shun these new ideas with confidence and the support of a very successful training group. Our top canoes and women were doubtful of these new ideas. They had years of top-level results to back their now proven techniques and many became naysayers of this new style. In the end most went back to the way they had paddled before.

Out West, on the other hand, we were isolated and trained every day with the desperate fear that other training groups would master these skills before we did. We were kayaks of a losing heritage who were desperately seeking a change for the better. We also knew a good thing when we saw it and had immediately seen the virtues of Jean-Michele's style. We knew the key to staying ahead of the pack would be to make the change quickly. Having said that, learning to paddle in an almost entirely new way was frustrating and hard. Skills that I had mastered long ago now seemed virtually impossibly hard and had to be re-learned all over again. That summer I had once finished eight spots from the best in the World but had, for a period of five or six months, thrown that away to start again from square one.

We were on to something and we knew it. In fact, we were on to a lot of things. The dynamic within our training group had become fantastic. Only twice in my life have I been a part of a training group that worked as well as our group out in Canada. At the time that group came together in 1991 not one men's kayak from North America had ever placed better than fifth in a single World Championship. Since that time the combined group of Canadian Dave Ford, Rich Weiss, and myself have amassed five individual medals in four World Championships.

The incredible thing about our American group, despite isolated camps such as our week spent with Jean-Michelle, was that we were largely coachless. It was a liability we didn't let limit our training one bit. We became our own coaches. We set out a yearly schedule in the fall and then met almost weekly to evaluate our training and set a weekly schedule. We held a fall training camp each year where we completely broke down our technique and then put it back together. We had winter camps to wet our appetite for racing and spring camps to refine those skills. Our appetite for the perfect workout was insatiable. In addition to our three regular short-course workouts a week we would have a fourth "coached" session that was designed and run by a different athlete each week. That athlete decided what to work on, set the gates and ran the workout with the idea of learning a specific skill.

Rich and I complemented each other perfectly in the workouts. Rich was a four-time state-wrestling champion and worked like a horse. He was consummate power and consistency. I was the glider. Where Rich would favor his arms I would cruise through on my edges, where I was a sitting duck on my edges Rich would power past me. In the end we both melded our strengths somewhere in the middle. By 1992 both Rich and I were poking fun at the other for having taken the other's style too far.

The one thing Rich brought to those workouts that I had never seen before was an unparalleled ability to train. All through my time as a junior I was the workhorse on the team. I trained twice daily and refused to be beaten in those workouts. Rich stunned me in our first workout together. He

absolutely left me standing still. I quickly exhausted myself just trying to prevent Rich from passing me on every repetition. By the time we were finished I had to climb out onto shore to lie down from exhaustion. It was at this point that Rich offered to design the next course. I kid you not, Rich was only half done with the workout! In the three years we trained together Rich and I did 13 grueling workouts a week. We took one rest day every two weeks and we never took a vacation. In all that time I only once heard Rich mention that he was tired. One single time!

Toughness became a mantra among us. Where we could have worn dry suits and pogies to keep warm we went barehanded and wore simple nylon paddle-jackets. Year round we arrived at our workouts barefoot and wearing shorts. When the weather turned especially wicked and cold, a time when other paddlers in other places might choose to stay inside in lieu of a whitewater workout, we resolutely arrived fifteen-minutes early to allow extra time to de-ice the

wires as we adjusted the gates. On one especially memorable day Rich and I returned to find my car entrapped in a wall of ice thrown up by a passing snowplow. Never one to tarry, Rich immediately jumped to the task of digging a passage through the snow mound with his kayak paddle. For five minutes we worked to dig a sufficient gap for my car to exit the parking lot. We stood barefoot in the snow throughout the entire task despite being less than ten feet from our dry clothes and snow boots.

Our toughness had a profound effect on our training. Despite the harsh Canadian winters our training totals were completely unaffected by the weather. If our training schedule said train, we trained; the weather had nothing to do with it. Our mindset became one of our biggest strengths. No amount of effort was too much to ask if it might pry precious milliseconds off our times. We were of singular mind and indefatigable in our efforts—we had become the purest form of fanatics.

We pushed the edge of the envelope in every way possible. This is especially true if you look at the whitewater we were running. The three of us, Brian Brown in particular, were making big and steep whitewater a regular part of our weekly training. The Chilliwack River will flood to biblical levels on a monthly basis throughout the winter. These floods would obliterate our slalom course, flood all of our eddys and make organized training an impossibility. For many this meant a week spent in the flatwater gates but for us it was a play day. We would race to the upper-Chilliwack canyon the next day and spend four hours in big water class four with our slalom boats. In the three years I trained with that group we consistently ran the biggest and most intimidating rivers we could find on a regular basis. In fact, we often would go out of our way to find an excuse to skip the gate training and go river running.

For those few years we were some of the best extreme boaters in the world. We were running any and everything with a confidence that soon began to outweigh our skills and our equipment. We ran flooded raging rivers and tight, steep, waterfall-laden creeks all in our eighteen-pound slalom kayaks. We knew we were on the ragged edge because the farther we went the more we began to falter. I had almost drowned on a tree in the upper canyon, Brian had pinned so badly that one of us had to swim out to rescue him, and Rich had one of the ugliest pins any of us had ever seen while playing in a C-1 at our training site. Yet still the shell of our invincibility remained un-cracked, for now.

In lieu of a flood we would often wake up early for a "Skook-Day"—a trip to the Skookumchuck narrows. This is a tidal riff north of Vancouver, B.C. that creates the greatest surfing wave in the world. I read once that the D.C. C-1s claimed that surfing the big wave at "O-deck" on the Potomac River of Maryland was the secret to their success. The Skook was O-deck on a heavy dose of steroids and most days we had it all to ourselves. The wave is easily thirty-five feet across and can build up to heights approaching eight to ten feet before it finally collapses into a monstrous hole. The wave was big enough that two people in slalom boats could swap sides while surfing the wave! This was slalom training at its best.

The three of us, along with several or our Canadian training partners, would make regular pilgrimages there. It was the most fun any of us ever had in a boat. We surfed for hour after hour and laughed the entire time. It was crazy, fast, powerful and challenging and most of all it was harmless. I often think back to those early days and the desperate attempts we were making to become champions. We went through a lot together, some good times and some bad. It is hard to think of any better memories than the those days at the Skook with Brian, Rich, and the Canadians.

I think it must be hard to believe how poor we were in those days. We lacked coaches, we lacked funding, we didn't even have the money for proper housing. The first winter I spent in Chilliwack I lived on the $1200 the USOC had given me for being the top

Junior the previous year. I lived in a broken down shoddy old tree house for $30 a month. I had no heat, no lights, and no running water. Top Canadian paddler Larry Norman was my neighbor and we shared a port-a-potty for a bathroom and cooked in an outdoor kitchen throughout the Canadian winter.

In many ways I began to feel like the deep-sea life I had studied in my high-school biology class. There is an entire ecosystem of sea life that is able to live far beneath the sea. At these depths they are out of reach of the sun's energy. Instead they exist on thermal energy supplied from geothermal vents on the Ocean floor. This was our situation in Chilliwack. We had no viable conventional heat source. Our only real source of heat was a shower/bath facility installed for summer rafters to bathe in after their trip down the river. This became our thermal vent and we crowded it for every joule of energy available.

At night we'd hang our wet gear on the rail with hopes it would dry by morning. Most nights the gear would freeze before it had a chance to drip dry. Even before we'd finished our dinners the gear was frozen stiff beyond any hope of being wearable. In the morning we'd fill a tub with hot water and drop the clothes in to thaw before we climbed in after them to get dressed. More often then not we'd do our workout and rush back to that same tub, our only real source of heat, to thaw out our frozen hands and feet as well as our clothes.

In the larger picture, despite the hardships, this was good training and it paid off with good results. In 1991 Rich was third in the Over-all World Cup and both David Ford and I finished in the top ten. By the next year Rich, Dave, and I had each won a World Cup race. We had a great training group and once again, as it had with the D.C. canoes, this dynamic was producing medals. We had taken North American kayaks and put them on the medals stand for the first time ever. I think there were a few things in particular that directly led to our success:

Rich, Brian and I worked with Mike Druice and Jean-Michele Prono on occasion, but probably did 98% of our training without a coach. Instead of being criticized by a coach we became very critical of each other's paddling. This is a rare trait among competitive training groups since constructive criticism does not mix well with elite-level egos. We, however, were able to put our pride aside and thus thrived on each other's advice. Each time one or the other of us would win a particular course we would decide between us why that was. It was like having three top-ten in the world coaches at the same workout.

We were also very competitive. I cannot remember a single non-competitive workout between the three of us. It is common now to be in a workout where people will suggest that this endurance set was going to be a "cruise". This was never once the case in our group. If Rich, Brian, or I were on the water we were on it to win, end of story. The idea was laughable to us at the time. We were competitive in every way, if one of us designed a hard course, the other would design a harder one. By the end of some workouts we would be doing moves that were often unimaginable at the beginning. If we had a technique workout we'd strive to have the best technique. If we had a sprint workout we'd launch ourselves out at full-pace every single run, and in the case of an endurance workout, particularly with Rich, we'd puke up a lung before we gave in. In short, if you lined up at a starting line with Rich, Brian, or I it was a race and we were going to try and beat you. If you wanted to go for a cruise, do it on your own time.

Lastly we were innovative and constantly seeking new ways to paddle faster. The one lesson we had learned well after failing at our first World Cup was that we didn't yet know how to beat these Europeans. The thirst for this knowledge became our crusade and we hired anyone and everyone to coach us for little mini-camps around the world. We also began to experiment with our regimented training plan to try and train the skills like edge control and timing that seemed to define the great paddlers. We had some workouts where we paddled more than half the workout as a C-1, others where we tried to take as few a number of strokes as possible. We took the disadvantage of only having a coach part-time and thrived on it. Every time we learned something new we'd take it back to the group and pick it apart until we had mastered it.

The real thread that ran through all of our training was responsibility. We took responsibility for ourselves in a way that is difficult to manage in a coached environment. Coached athletes often leave it up to their coach to decide which skills to learn, when and how hard to train, and most of all to evaluate their performance. We took responsibility for these things ourselves and thus had the most demanding coach possible. No coach could, in good conscience, have asked their athletes to go through the things we went through those years. We were fanatics beyond what a reasonable person can imagine.

We were fanatics chasing a single carrot on a single stick. Our objective was the Barcelona Olympics and our proving grounds were the 1992 U.S. Olympic Team trials appropriately held on the Savage River. The countdown to the trials had begun long before we heard the ticking of the clock but as the date drew near not a single moment of time's passing went unnoticed.

There are many in this world who consider themselves athletes. Across America these "athletes" test themselves weekly on the soccer and football fields of our high schools and colleges. They claim to have tested their mettle in homecoming victories and regional championships but they have only scraped the surface of our world. Win or lose they will miss not a moment of their daily lives. After the game they will continue on with school or their jobs and leave their homes each morning reassured by the well-trod path they follow. Only their pride was on the line.

Not so in the brotherhood of the would-be Olympian. We set aside our school and drained our bank accounts. There is no pressure quite so palpable as that which comes from investing your entire being in one single event. Imagine taking everything you ever owned into a stadium filled with people you

never met. Imagine standing on a pile of your worldly goods and challenging that crowd to a test. Imagine offering everything you own to the person there who could beat you. Still you have only scratched the surface of what we stood to lose at those Olympic trials.

The pressure builds slowly throughout the year. At first it is embodied as stress. In the late fall and early winter I began to worry that my competitors were training harder or better than I was. I would constantly redouble my efforts during workouts to make sure no one could outdo my training. Later it becomes a worry, the late winter and early spring were filled with worry. Every bad workout or lost competition would leave me sleepless as I tossed and turned over my uncertain future. Finally, by spring it had become fear. I was afraid of missing that team and that fear left my training partners and I constantly on edge. It was common to see one of us break out in a tantrum because of one bad run through a training course. The team trials are a make or break competition—a loss here is the end of the road for so many who had made the claim of "Olympic Hopeful".

## The 1992 Olympics

My memories of those first Olympic trials are like a slide show in my head. I don't remember a single sound from that race, just vividly clear vignettes of the events as they transpired. I remember putting in far upstream of my competitors. I had spent most of my life training alone and there was comfort in being alone here. The Savage River was coated once again in a low level of fog and its veil energized me. I remember feeling alternately invincibly strong and vulnerably scared.

The strength came from the knowledge that I could have done no more than I had to prepare for this race. The terror came from gate one. Ask anyone who was there about the 1992 Olympic trials and

Photo by Chris Smith.

they'll talk about the first two gates. In twenty years of racing they remain the most difficult beginning to a race I have ever seen. Right from the start there was a tricky six-second lead in to gate one. The paddler had to work his way straight down out of an eddy and along a row of rocks towards a medium sized hydraulic just below. Just as the athletes passed through the first gate they were required to hook off of the corner of this hole, across its top in a balancing act that rivaled the greatest gymnasts, and wind up surfing the wave on the far side into an upstream gate two. As I awaited my start with the final few paddlers, I sat in plain view of these two gates but avoided watching my competitors negotiate this tricky combination. There were more than a few paddlers who would wash away years of training in the first six seconds of this competition.

Olympic trials, like no other event, are the coldest most inhumane and most definitively final event in sports today. Many here today had missed selection to the National team many times in the past few years but were able to shrug it off and continue preparing for this event. Those trials were but a stepping-stone to this final destination, a bump in the road for their Olympic preparations. These Olympic trials were different; failure here meant retirement for many. This was the end of the road for many deserving athletes.

I had always pictured the Olympic trials the way it is portrayed on television—a glorious day filled with the thrill of victory. This was never the case for me. It is a day filled with tears and sadness. It is truly a day of kill or be killed. Making the team seems more like a relief than a victory. Watching your friends and teammates miss that same team is heartbreaking. Partnerships that had shaped my life were split in those few short hours of competition on the Savage River. Rich Weiss and I won our spots on the U.S. Olympic team. After fifteen years of training I had finally become an Olympian. My friend and training partner Brian Brown would not, he had

Photo by Ken Redmond.

missed that final spot. In more than ten years of trying this was the first time he had ever missed the National Team.

The stress we experienced in the months leading up to these trials had caused many troubles between my teammates. We had one especially outspoken teammate who was constantly railing on the coaches to ensure he had the best support available at the Games. He had railed about everything from adequate housing to an unfair schedule that required us to give up a night's sleep for the chance to march in the Opening Ceremonies. At one point this teammate had loudly proclaimed, "I'm not going to that parade." It was a criticism our assistant coach took patiently in stride, one of many difficult moments he would have to bear in the following months.

I remember watching in shock as this same teammate took a fatal penalty on the final day of competition. I was stunned to realize that this great paddler would not be going to the Games with us. I turned a confused eye to this same assistant coach who stood behind me on the bridge. Once again he had the same patient look on his face as he again took this news in stride. Under his breath I heard him say to no one in particular "That's right, you're not going to the parade!"

Making the Olympic team is both a relief from and a continuation of the same sort of pressure I'd been feeling so much of lately. I was relieved to have made it through that first hurdle but I also had begun to feel the same need to train harder and prepare more for the upcoming Olympics. Rich and I had already laid out our training plans through the Games so both of us hit the ground running. Our immediate plans were to head directly to Spain for a couple of weeks training on the Olympic course itself before doing a single World Cup race in England and then returning home for a solid training cycle on our home waters at Chilliwack.

The Nottingham race was a bit of a quandary for me. On the one hand it was the only big World Cup Race that year. Everyone who was to compete in the Games was expected to use this as their last test race. On the other hand this was the home course of the elite British kayak team. Led by many time World Champion Richard Fox this squad consisted of no less than four separate World or World Championship medallists. Looking at it rationally I knew that you pick your fights and this wasn't the one for me. On the flip side, skipping races is for pansies—necessary arrogance.

My late entry into the race left me once again at the start of the pack. I was one of the first off the line, more than an hour ahead of the British Squad. The course, despite being set on what can barely be described as whitewater, was tricky and hard. Some race runs everything comes together and it feels like you are invincible. You are neither tired, nor rushed; you are infallible. My race run in Nottingham that year was just that. I finished the run, shook off the sudden wave of fatigue I felt after my run and then began an easy warm down. I remember thinking, "Good run; not so fast." All my great runs felt that way, like the gates weren't coming at me fast enough and like I hadn't paddled hard enough. I spent the rest of the day in feverish worry that someone would best my score.

Nobody did, And I had my first World Cup win. After two full World Cups and a World Championship—eleven agonizing races without a medal—I had earned a berth on the medal's stand. This was vindication at last. I don't know how many times in the last two years I had wondered if I would ever medal in a race. Nottingham was the barometer by which all of us tested our readiness for the Barcelona Games.

You are really an Olympian for such a short time. After our trip to Europe Rich and I returned home to a month's hard training in Chilliwack. Each day I woke up an Olympian and yet was discouraged to find my day was very much the same as any other. I wanted to scream out to any and everyone that I was going to the Olympics but there was no one there to shout it to. The Canadians were off training abroad and Rich and I were left home to train by ourselves.

The Games truly begin when you climb off the plane at team processing. It was like crossing through the gateway to another world. Several of us flew down to Miami on the same flight from D.C. for team processing. This is an intense two days of being briefed on and dressed up as Olympic athletes. Not long before I had been living in a tree house and wearing the same wardrobe I had worn in high school. Here we were put up in the Hilton and given three full suitcases of new clothes and equipment.

The whole of team process is a bizarre orgy of giving that is some sort of exponential expansion of a two-hour shopping spree being multiplied by all of your Christmases put together. You fly in one night and are met at the airport. Somebody takes care of your luggage and somebody gets your boats so that you can be expressed back to the hotel for a fine steak dinner. After a good night's sleep in a queen size bed you are softly awakened for a buffet breakfast—the Hilton has a large supply of fresh linens in case you'd like to bathe first. After sharing breakfast with everyone from speed walkers to gold medal swimmers you are ushered into a large room and given a gigantic shopping cart. Let the orgy begin.

The room is like a warehouse filled with shelves and tables around its perimeter. You go to each of these tables and simply offer them the size of clothes you wear. They check your name off the list and fill your cart with treasure. Ten or twelve shirts, three pairs of new shoes, new camera, new alarm clock, and three pairs of pants to go with your four pairs of shorts. Any and everything fills your cart. Somewhere along the way you adopt a Cabbage Patch doll, get a massage, have your teeth checked for lurking cavities, and later cough twice to check for hernias.

This was the sort of booty pirates had written shanties about and we whipped ourselves into a feverish feeding frenzy. I ran from table to table getting anything they had to offer; free shaving cream that I wouldn't need for years to come, cologne that I wouldn't wear even if I were anonymous, tampons

and hairdryers. We were sharks who smelled blood and didn't care if we were getting fine tuna or some putrid tourist wrapped in neoprene. At one point a gargantuan decathlete pointed at the shorts my coach was wearing and demanded to know where they came from. "I didn't get any of those!" he demanded. "I brought them", my coach replied as he continued to dress.

Our flight to Spain was even more crazy. It was like an airborne dinner party. It was an entire Boeing 767 filled with Olympic athletes. The plane had no more than taken off before we were all wandering the aisles to meet people. This was the greatest collection of American athletes of the entire quadrenium and we wandered from seat to seat as we got to know them. Movies played non-stop on the video screens and we could request a meal anytime we liked. By the time of our arrival we had become such a rowdy bunch that the request to take our seats resulted in a mammoth pillow fight that didn't end until we pulled up to our gate on the ground.

Our excitement was infectious. Every new discovery was an uncovered wonderland. The Olympic Village was a step above club med. It boasted a private beach in downtown Barcelona, a video game hall built to host 10,000 athletes, a boardwalk, a dining hall with food from every corner of the world, and for us Americans, a McDonalds. I felt like a Neanderthal who had just been chipped out of a Canadian glacier and had awakened to discover a whole new world.

Despite the distractions we also had to get down to business. The Olympics eat away at your training time and I was struggling to stick to a training plan that didn't fit my surroundings. The organizing committee opened the gates for training just after our arrival with the U.S. squad but promised to close it a full five days before I began my race runs. Our team had laid out plans to do an extended camp here at the Olympic course, take a short break at a training camp in nearby France, and then train a couple more days on the course before being sidelined till the race.

My carefully laid training plans began to fall in shambles. I felt pulled this way and that by the different events that surround the Olympics. I was quickly injured after arriving from the U.S. and had to take three days off with a strained rib. Soon after I was rushing to catch up with my missed training and wore myself out to the point where my training was visibly ineffective. I took a break long enough to climb in a car and head to France for our organized break. In essence I felt like I was spinning my wheels and getting nowhere fast.

I tried desperately to take charge of my training. I skipped the Opening Ceremonies in favor of the sleep I felt I needed. I removed myself from the team training plan and began to focus on moves and courses that I felt were important. In short I was trying to find some sort of balance to the whirlwind of the Olympics around me.

In the middle of all of this the race sort of snuck up on me. I remember sleeping poorly the night before my event and feeling a bit dazed throughout the day. My first run was extremely poor. I just couldn't seem to get the boat moving. On my second run I finally found my groove. I was aggressive, sharp and crisp. It was the kind of run where nothing could go wrong and then it did. I was the fastest to gate thirteen and the fastest from gate thirteen to the finish. I had a great run except that I had missed that gate. Ten inches off line and my Olympic dreams were finished.

I had never realized until then how completely I had convinced myself that I would one day be the Olympic champion. That loss was the kind of crushing defeat that still hurts ten years later. An Olympic failure is utter and complete defeat. Perhaps in the eyes of those you know—those who truly matter in your life—you have accomplished something. To the rest of America any result outside the medals is a defeat.

My most painful memory after those Games was returning straight home for a race series in the Midwest. We had a race in South Bend, Indiana and I was coincidentally billeted with the same family that Italian Pierpalo Ferrazi had stayed with the year before. Pierpalo was now the Olympic Champion and my hosts were more proud of him than if he had been their own son. At one point I had arranged to meet training partners the next day at one o'clock for a mid-day workout. My host looked surprised at our late start and commented, "Pierpalo always got up at six in the morning to train...maybe that's why he won".

It was like a stab to the heart. I wanted to scream. I wanted to shout out about all the icy workouts and frozen clothes. I wanted to scream about chasing Rich—who might as well have been a training machine—for thousands of hours of endurance workouts. I wanted to explain what it felt like to train so hard your lungs burned and you vomit on the deck of your boat before doing another run, another rep, another set. I had given everything I had for that medal; I had dropped out of school, I had lived on rice and beans in a frozen tree-house, I had seen my family only in passing as I traveled from one training site to another. I wanted to scream all these things she would never understand.

## The Aftermath

Our training group eventually began to fall apart. Brian missed the 1992 Olympic team. Rich and I both competed there but failed to medal. Those Games were essentially the end of our group. Brian retired, Rich kept training but moved back to school and I remained in Chilliwack, desperate to make up for my poor performance at the Barcelona Games.

My training situation changed dramatically. Rich and I would still train together on weekends but I was often away on training trips to Costa Rica or the East coast. Ironically, the year following the Games was our best year in terms of results: Rich was second at the World Championships and I finally won the World Cup. I had left the Olympics the previous year saddened that we had improved so much and accomplished so little at the Games. That World Cup

was my redemption. No more hanging my head in shame after telling people I had finished twenty-seventh at the Games. I had transformed myself from Olympic loser to Olympic hopeful once again.

Maybe it was these titles that got in our way or maybe it was just time to move on but for the most part Rich and I quit training together except in camps and at races. Although we never had one specific disagreement we did grow apart. By the time the 1996 Games rolled around we were still friendly to each other but never met outside of our team workouts. It was the sort of tension that I felt grew naturally with the stress of the Games and also the sort of tension that I was sure would disappear after they were over. Like a lot of disagreements at big races I was sure this one would fade away with time. This was not to be the case. Eleven months after finishing fifth at the Atlanta Olympics Rich Weiss drowned at the base of a waterfall on the White Salmon River in the state of Washington. He left behind many who miss him and I hope his legacy shines from the pages of this book

## Fall Training

For the four years between the Barcelona Games and the Atlanta Games my training began to take on a cadence that I found to be particularly effective for winning races. I would come home from the last race at the end of the summer and begin my training right away—I was never much on training breaks. I felt that it was important to begin the weights and fitness work early—before I began to train in earnest in the boat again. This way I wasn't dealing with soreness during my long endurance workouts. I would intersperse this fitness training with mammoth doses of river running and surf expeditions. I never wandered far from the big water days I had spent on the Chilliwack.

In the late fall I was mixing that fitness with large amounts of endurance training. My week would include six to seven long endurance or lactic endurance workouts alongside the weights and running. The remaining workouts were focused on learning new technique. One lesson I had learned during my dismal races of 1989 had been to never be content with my current level of ability. I had spent the entire year in 1989 trying to repeat my training workout for workout from the year before and had failed because of it. From that point on I had focused on trying something new every single year. I felt that the act of learning new technique and trying new approaches to training was what gave my training an edge. Even if I decided that the experiment was a failure the act of trying it had expanded my abilities and kept my training fresh and challenging. For example I would change the way I did offsets or upstreams for a month and then compare it to my old method. Off and on through the years I've tried hundreds of different ideas from ice baths to C-1 paddling mostly just to keep the flow of ideas in my training alive.

As soon as I could afford to I began to make a

habit of going away in the winter. The sort of training I was getting in the warm sun of Costa Rica just wasn't possible in the harsh environment of Canada. In Chilliwack we jumped on the water and did the prescribed workout and then raced back to our cars to get warm. Often the challenge of training to be the best was dwarfed by the challenge of surviving the elements. In Costa Rica I was able to spend hours of extra time tweaking different parts of my technique and playing in the gates.

In addition, I felt like the quality of my paddling would always decrease over the first part of the winter. In the course of doing all the long endurance and the large workload I would tend to slouch more and not make my turns as crisply. These Southern training camps gave me the chance to work some of these kinks out as well as getting some of my first quality race-length workouts in.

## Spring Sparring Sessions

Keeping a real feel for where I was throughout the year was important to my training program. I knew that I would get slower in the fall while I did my long slow training and that this would improve slightly through the winter as I began to work a little more specifically on my racing. I tried to avoid racing during these times because I knew the temptation would be there to break from my training plan to improve my performance in those unimportant events. However, in the early spring I would make a point of training with someone from the top-ten in the world. These "sparring sessions," as I thought of them, would both hone my high-speed racing technique and give me a reality check about where I was in relation to my international competition. If I found I was slower than the people I trained with I still had two to three months with which to make improvements.

I missed having that elite group at Chilliwack to spar against. In those early years we had had all the competition we could stand living within ten minutes of each other. After that group broke up following the Barcelona Games I found I often had to travel quite far to find the same sort of environment. These trips were often quite rewarding though. In 1995 I had traveled to England to train with Shaun Pierce and Ian Raspin after their successful World Cup campaigns the year before but found much more there than just these two paddlers. Great athletes seldom train in a vacuum. Behind these two top paddlers was a highly motivated training group that came from the same vein as both our Chilliwack group and the D.C. C-1s. The training there was fantastic.

Off and on over the next five years I would do spring training with top-ten athletes from over ten different countries! These spring camps became an annual part of my training. You simply have to have great competition to have great training. I felt like so many athletes are surprised at the first World Cup race every year. Often they discover that they were not on pace to medal at these early races. I arrived at the first World Cup every year sure of the fact that I could win (between 1996 and 2000 I won the first race three out of five times, only failing to medal once by finishing fourth). These early racing camps served as my yearly "barometer" so that I could gage my abilities well in advance.

## Racing versus Training

I began to think of my racing season as a balance between performance at the individual races and my overall fitness. Some seasons I would race every weekend and invariably would see my performance drop over the course of the summer. I found that if I tried to train through these races my performance on the weekends would be far below par. In the end I decided on two things. First, I would have to race less. Often I would only do a few races a season outside of the World Cup so that I could maintain my fitness for these or other important races.

Photo by Scott Shipley.

**1987 U.S. TEAM MEMBER
DOUG GORDON**
Photo by Jamie McEwan.

The other thing I began to do was force myself to train through these race series. I made it a goal to do a large volume of work on the Monday and Tuesday following a big event. This way I would get some fitness work in but still leave time to taper through the rest of the week in preparation for the weekend races.

Many of the characteristics of those early days in Chilliwack permeated my training throughout my career. Certainly the work ethic, our competitive nature and our methodical approach to technique remained. More surprisingly some of what we thought of as our liabilities also remained. With the exception of the 1996 and the 2000 seasons I remained primarily coachless, choosing instead to seek out coaching for a month, a week, or less. I made it a priority to work with as many different coaches as possible to learn new ideas, but then assimilated those ideas into my training for the remainder of the time.

In a lot of ways my search for coaching was not dissimilar to my search for training partners. I sought out the best coaches and worked with them in an intense training environment. I had the chance to work with Jean-Michele Prono, the Frenchman who coached three ladies onto the medal stand in 1993. I also worked with Richard and Myriam Fox many time World Champions between them. When Paul Rattcliffe became the fastest kayak in the World I turned to his coach and my friend, Jimmy Jayes, to find out how. In course of the last eight years of my career I worked with an uncountable number of coaches in addition to Sylvan Poberaj and Bob Campbell from the U.S. staff. I felt like it was the US coaches who helped make me a fast racer. They knew my style, knew my training schedule and knew enough about me to help me both in my preparation and my races. But I felt that it was the outside coaching, the people I worked with from other countries, who brought in new ideas and kept my training dynamic.

While I tried to vary the particulars of my training from year to year this was the essential method I followed from 1993 through the Sydney Games with basically excellent results. The technique I learned from these coaches and the way I practiced and honed that technique through the year made for crushingly consistent results. In the eight years following the Barcelona Games I finished top two in the over-all World Cup every single year. That's an 100% medal rate! I finished second in three of those four World Championships (Rich was second in the remaining event) and never lost a National Championship.

Our original training group has had similar results. What had started as a small group of incredibly keen athletes in one of the far corners of the world had become an elite group of successful racers. We had finally come of age, lived our time at the top to its fullest and have now come to our twilight. As with so many other athletes our era has come to an end and with it, my racing career.

Like the D.C. C-1s my time has come and passed. The sum of my knowledge and experience is in this book. I brought to the world of whitewater slalom a consistent intensity that I hope flows from these pages into another generation of paddlers as did the exploits of Lugbill, Fox, and the Hearns into mine. In the sum of my career I was never an Olympic Champion as were none of those paddlers I idolized so early on in my paddling. Like them I am content with my World Cup and World Championship victories. Like them I take pride neither in the results themselves nor the medals I've brought home, but in the efforts that preceded them. I hang my hat not on that final destination but on every crushing stroke it took to reach it.

# Technique

*"The people who win aren't just faster, they are better. They are better and they know more. When I watch the best paddlers, Paul Rattcliffe or Scott Shipley, I see their strokes not just pushing or turning the boat, but putting it in exactly the right place"*

*-Sylvan Poberaj, U.S. Olympic Team Coach*

## The Strokes

Whitewater slalom, particularly the pursuit of excellence in whitewater slalom, is a path fraught with many challenges. Ours is a sport that demands so much of an athlete just to survive the trip down the river. Remember that there are hundreds of thousands of people each year who are challenged enough to simply paddle down a river much less perform at the level to which you are aspiring. Becoming a great slalom athlete will demand that you train your body, both physically and mentally, to the limit of your ability.

Perhaps the greatest challenge of our sport is the technical. The strongest and fittest paddlers are not necessarily the ones who top the results lists. Races are won by slalomists—the ones who have done more than simply trained and retrained the basic elements of stroke and gate technique. For these athletes there is more to slalom than simply combining the strokes and leans of basic boat control into the lines and turns of a slalom course. For these athletes slalom is a dance, alternately gliding with the finesse of a ballerina or exploding with the power of a jaguar.

This is true of top athletes in almost every sport. There is a fluidity of motion-something that is virtually indescribable-about their efforts. Their prowess is best described as "Something Special," as in "There is something special about the way they do that." There are many reasons why these top athletes are special but much of it can be boiled down to a few simple building blocks. Top athletes have spent hours inventing and working on stroke drills that emphasize these foundations-simply learning good stroke or gate technique is not enough. Elite paddling is taking the basic mechanics of good stoke technique and weaving a dance out of it.

Many look at great athletes and see a "gift" in the special way that they perform. At the peak of any sport there is a pack of athletes whom are above all others-the brotherhood (or sisterhood) of the gifted. It takes more than just work to join this elite group-you must paddle like a champion. Former U.S.

Olympic coach Bill Endicott once said that the difference between being great or simply good in canoe slalom came down to five major differences. Regardless of how well you master the mechanics of your stroke and gate technique your true objective lies in this short list.

**Balance:** The great paddlers have all been supremely comfortable in the setting of a boat. Their paddling is characterized by smooth firm leans and the confidence to contort or extend their boats and bodies into any imaginable position.

**Extension:** Top paddlers are flexible and confident enough to work within the entire range of their reach. These paddlers fully rotate, extend, and execute their strokes with the ideal blade placement and maximum extension.

**Combinations of forces:** Another name for this is "coordination." The best paddlers coordinate their entire body into making each stroke. Each muscle fires in coordination with all the rest such that a steady crushing force is applied in a controlled yet explosive manner.

**No extraneous movements:** The best paddlers are also the most efficient. These are not the paddlers with their faces squished up in a mask of pain and they are not the paddlers who bob and nip and duck with each stroke. Every stroke is a combination of the necessary elements for that stroke and nothing more.

**Speed of prime movers:** The best paddlers simply execute good technique faster and more cleanly than the rest. This can be thought of as the combination of the preceding four points. Once you have mastered those you will have the balance, the leverage, the coordination and the efficiency to truly move like a champion. I can remember watching Richard Fox hit gate one in his final run at the 1989 World Championships. what followed was a stunning display of the difference between Fox and the rest of us. What had been a steady controlled and precise Fox became a desperate frantic and controlled Fox! He was the picture of perfect technique yet he was scrambling to make up for lost time.

## Forward Stroke

The forward stroke is usually the hardest stroke to change. Almost every single one of us climbed into a kayak for the first time and, after a quick introduction, began paddling. Unfortunately, whatever mistakes we made in those first few strokes quickly became bad habits. Bad habits that, by the time you read this book, will have been practiced thousands and thousands of times to the point where you are sure you could never rid yourself of them. Keep this in mind though. Your forward stroke is the base that your race run rests on. Being able to quickly execute powerful and coordinated forward strokes is essential to a fast race run.

One thing you must believe when working on your forward stroke is that being fast across a lake does NOT mean you have a good stroke technique for slalom. The best stroke for whitewater is not the best stroke for wildwater, it is not the best stroke for flat-water racers and it is not the stroke that makes you go the fastest. A good slalom stroke allows for quick reactions from side to side, quick accelerations and is compatible enough with your other strokes that you can quickly switch from one to other. In short, you need a forward stroke that is a hybrid of your turning strokes. This way, in the event you are pushed off line, you can react quickly without switching from _propulsion mode_ to _control mode." When your forward stroke is perfected, your arms, shoulders and torso will mimic the motion of a forward sweep. Only the path and angle of your paddle should differ.

My first few years on the team I was always taught to _keep the paddle vertical," and to keep the blade, _close to the boat,_ so that each stroke efficiently pushed the boat straight ahead. The idea, which is true, was that any yawing, which is the tendency of the boat to wander off course with each stroke, was inefficient to a boat meant to go in a straight line. If the paddle was straight up and down and close to the centerline it was pushing the boat as directly forward as possible. We were also taught to punch, with our elbows out (bench-press and shot-put style), to lever the stroke about the lower pulling hand. Despite all my fitness and stroke work I found that in my first two years on the World Cup circuit that I often lost control and made mistakes every time I sped up through easier gate combinations. I was losing races in the easy parts! I simply could not control my boat in whitewater with a high stroke rate. I spent hours and hours working my basic gate technique before I realized that it was my stroke that was the problem! This "efficient" stroke gave me no control in whitewater! A vertical next-to-the-boat forward is unforgiving and unstable. What I needed was a forward stroke that was more stable and allowed me to react quickly when the boat strayed off course. The stroke I developed is based around these few basic guidelines.

A good forward stroke is powerful only if you are using your entire back, shoulders, torso, legs and arms at the same time. Think of this more as a coordinated spring forward than as a stiff and awkward twist. The effort must be coordinated such that each muscle involved in the stroke fires at the same time-a powerful stroke is a coordinated effort. This stroke rotates around the spine, meaning that the stroke side of your body will twist downstream while the opposite side will twist upstream. Here are some things to keep in mind:

**Sit up straight:** The lower vertebrate of your back need to be straight to rotate properly. This means that your lower back must be supported so that you can sit up. It can help to have a straight-backed seat and to consciously focus on sitting up straight.

**Rotate from the bottom of your torso:** Try and feel your one hip going forward and your other twisting back. It is easy to feel like you are using your back when in fact you are really only rotating your shoulders. Your whole back should twist and untwist at the same rate.

**Keep your elbows in:** There is a popular conception in paddling that you should keep your elbows out, or horizontal, while punching out your top arm. This mimics the position your arms naturally take in similar movements like shot-put or bench-press. The problem with this is that your forward sweep strokes need your elbows in, thus if you want to switch quickly from a forward stroke to a sweep you need to re-organize your arms. Better to have them in position right from the start.

**Reach:** The most important part of your forward strokes are the catch and initial pull. Optimize your strokes by making sure you are getting the most distance out of each stroke. Keep in mind though that you do NOT want to be bobbing your body! A forward stroke is a smooth, powerful rotation about your spine. You should be inserting the blade into the water as far forward as you can comfortably reach without bobbing or lunging for a few unneeded extra inches of reach.

When your forward stroke is perfected, your arms shoulders and torso will mimic the motion of the forward sweep. Photo by Chris Smith.

**Catch:** The _catch_ of the stroke, or how the blade first grabs the water is very important. If the blade slips you will lose a part of your stroke, and your effort, to splashing the water around. If you wait too long your stroke is unresponsive and not very quick. The trick is to immerse the entire blade at the start of the stroke before you pull on the blade! Once then entire blade is in the water snap your stroke from there. A good stroke should have virtually no splash off the blade and the boat should rocket forward.

**Recover:** As you pull the paddle through the water do not let your blade come past your hip. As the blade comes even with your body slide it out to the side while you simultaneously insert the other blade into the water at the beginning of its stroke. You will find that to do this you must not let your top hand, or "punching hand" cross the centerline of the boat. In a purely mechanical sense you should find that if that top "punching" hand does stray across the centerline of the boat it will force you to make a longer and less controllable stroke. I try and make an imaginary line between my eyes and the tip of my bow and then force myself to keep my punching hands on the outside of that line.

## Advanced

A good stroke, as shown on the left, carries away from the center of rotation while still pushing the water straight back and stops at the paddler's hip. A common mistake is to keep the paddle right beside the boat and let the stroke carry behind the paddler.

Start to think about where the center of rotation is for your boat. The center of rotation is the spot your boat tends to spin around when you turn the boat. For most paddlers this is right in front of the paddler's crotch, halfway to their knees. To turn the boat you need to get the blade away from that center of rotation. Think of it this way. If you could paddle right on the centerline of your boat you would almost effortlessly paddle in a straight line. The opposite is also true: if you can get a stroke as

**SIDEVIEWS OF GOOD STROKE**
A good forward stroke rotates about the spine, has long extension and a good catch, and finishes at the hip. Photo by Chris Smith.

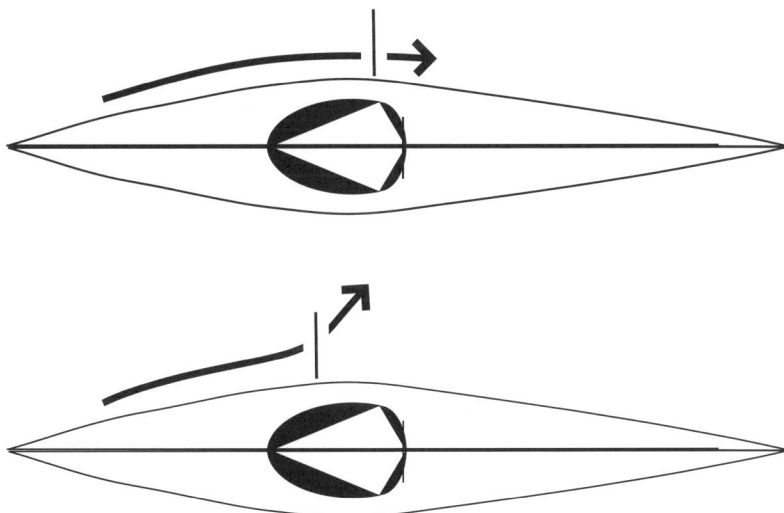

**PATH OF PADDLE**
The path of the paddle during a sweep stroke should be tailored to optimize your turn.

**HARD EARLY PART OF STROKE**
Pull hard immediately after the blade fully enters the water.
Photo by Chris Smith.

far as possible from that centerline, in fact from the point at the center of your turn, the boat will turn dramatically. A sweep that is inserted way out by the bow, and then follows a path in a wide arc away from the boat has quite a lot of lever arm and thus spins the boat quite quickly.

For a forward stroke to really offer you the sort of control needed for whitewater it actually needs a moment arm for control! In short, your forward stroke needs to stay away from the center of rotation of your boat so that you can make minute adjustments in your boats course.

Now that you have mastered the basic forward stroke, start to tailor the path of your forward stroke so that it always gives you some sort of moment arm about your center of rotation. Try this: put the blade in the water, next to the boat as you always do, and as far forward as you can comfortably reach. Then, as you pull the blade back through the water slice the paddle more out to the side. Then finish your stroke by sliding the blade out of the water, to the side, at your hip. The path of your blade should look like a "J" in the water although the power face will always face directly towards the stern.

The idea is this: if you were sprinting along through whitewater and were halfway through a stroke on the right when a boil came along and pushed the boat to the right. If the paddle were right up against the boat you would have to finish that stroke and take a stroke on the left, before you could straighten your boat with a sweep on the right. With your new stroke you can easily control the boat INSTANTLY by simply pulling harder or softer on the blade. Your forward stroke now has the control of a turning stroke!

### Elite

Now try and work on making your strokes quick, crisp, and powerful. Tests have shown that the most important part of your stroke is the first third, the part right after the catch but before the paddle reaches your knees. Now focus on applying your the

## TRY THIS DRILL:

Go out for a distance paddle on the lake at a moderate to easy pace. As you paddle across the lake take thirty seconds out of every minute to exaggerate the characteristics of a good stroke. When I do the workout it goes something like this:

* 4 minutes easy-medium paddling.
* 30" medium paddling while focusing on sitting up as straight as I can. I try and focus on pushing my head out the top of my spine.
* 30" medium paddling
* 30" medium paddling focusing on rotating as far as I can with each stroke. I exaggerate this stroke so much that my eyes, shoulder, elbow and top hand line up with each stroke before I put the blade in the water. I also exaggerate the use of my shoulders and back while I do this drill.
* 30" medium paddling
* 30" medium paddling focusing on reaching as far as I can. This drill is quite similar to the rotating drill except I am focusing on watching the blade cleanly catch as far forward as possible. I also focus on not "bobbing" my body. This stroke, even exaggerated, is a rotation only.
* 30" medium paddling
* 30" medium paddling focusing on keeping my elbows in. I also focus on the path of the stroke so that it is a neat little "J" as I describe in the "Advanced" section.
* 30" medium paddling
* Now I slowly count from one to ten as I paddle across the lake. With each increment I tighten every muscle, from my toes to my jaw, in my entire body. At 1, the beginning, I am completely relaxed but by the time I reach ten I am so tense I can barely reach out and take a stroke. Then I do the same thing in reverse from ten back down to one.
* 30" medium paddling
* Put it all together piece by piece. First I sit up as straight as I can, still highly exaggerated. Now I over-rotate and extend my reach. Next bring in the elbows and focus on the path of the paddle. You should feel as tense now as you did at the count of ten before. In your mind count down again from ten, relaxing your muscles—and your exaggeration—as you count down. When you reach about seven or six stop counting down. This should be a perfect forward stroke.
* 20 minutes medium-hard paddling across the lake.
* Rest 4 minutes and repeat

full power of your stroke right at the start. Be sure to get the blade cleanly and fully in the water at the catch and then instantly apply power to the stroke.

## Turning the boat

*"Scott, if you can master these three turns, you can do anything in a boat"*
*-Jean-Michelle Prono*
*French National Team Coach*

One of my favorite memories of racing was watching Britain's Richard Fox race at Bourg St. Maurice in 1991. Fox had an incredible race and I was awed by how he made such quick work of a difficult course. Fox was quick, concise, and precise the entire length of the course and won by a sizeable margin. What stuck out most for me was how incredible a particular upstream was. This particular upstream had a terrible approach that made getting a good approach angle very difficult. The eddyline was half hole and half eddy but had a terrific rip on the outside. It was an upstream that gave virtually everyone in the race trouble yet Fox nipped in and out of there like it was a flatwater upstream. What was it that made such a gate so easy for Fox? Everyone has a hot flash here or there yet Fox managed to nail this particular combination three times in a row. Why is it that he was so successful when others were not?

Trying to learn to mimic another paddler on such difficult maneuver will make your pursuit of excellence last a lifetime. Each turn has so many nuances that make it unique and, unfortunately, from the perspective of the paddler, intricate. It seems like there are a million different ways for a paddler to turn a boat. Luckily there is an easier way to break it down. A kayak, as a boat, can only turn four different ways. It can slide, carve, pivot, or bank. Before you work on perfecting your turning strokes be sure you understand what these four things are. Every turn you make in slalom will be some combination of these four maneuvers. Even in the trickiest of upstreams where the top boats are using dramatic leans and lunging intricate strokes you will see that the boats are doing some simple combination of these four turns. To many people this way of looking at it may seem oversimplified but keep in mind what the French coach Jean-Michele Prono told me when I was 19 (Note that it was understood that anyone can bank a boat), _Scott, if you can master these three turns you can do anything in a boat_. I look at it this way, you can spend an eternity learning to mimic every intricate stroke for every unique gate, or you can learn to think of every move on a slalom course as a simple combination of one or all of these four simple turns.

**The Sliding Turn:** is turning the boat without heading in the direction of your turn and without sinking either end. This is the equivalent to a hockey stop in skating or a skid stop in skiing. On flatwater you can do this turn by spinning your boat round and round in one place without going anywhere at all and without pivoting. In a race it is often used to turn the boat and give it the necessary angle even when you don't necessarily want to charge the boat in that direction.

**A Carving Turn:** is just the opposite of sliding. Carving is when you use the edges of the boat as a skeg to keep the stern from sliding and thus carry speed through your turn. Basically what you are doing is keeping the boat moving through an arc. This is turning and going at the same time by leaning away from your turn and using that edge to keep the boat from sliding out. This is often the most efficient way to keep up your speed while still maneuvering through the course.

**The Pivot Turn:** is a quick sit-and-spin maneuver used to spin the boat quickly IN ONE PLACE. It is the save of all saves as you can often turn against the current, in narrow positions, or else use this turn to completely reverse directions. Most medium level slalom racers depend on this turn almost exclusively on a race run which can be a disastrous waste of time. The pivot turn is the showboat of all turns in that it looks good and feels good. Unfortunately it takes a lot of energy and stops the boat for a part of the turn. Keep in mind that if you stand that boat on end it cannot move relative to the water it is in. I was stunned once at a World Cup in Lofer after a run where I cranked out an aggressive and dynamic pivot through the crux move on the course. The move was so flashy that Eurosport used it as a background for all their bulletins throughout the race. I was awed later when I took splits against a young German paddler who slid in and out of the gate with a timid wiggle merely sliding the boat instead of pivoting. Not only was he faster but he took a full second out of what I considered a perfect gate! Later that young paddler, Oliver Fix, would go on to win the World Championships and the Olympics.

**The Bank Turn:** This is also known as the inside lean. This is the maneuver of simply leaning into

**PIVOTING TURN**
A pivot turn is used to quickly turn the boat in one place. Photo by Chris Smith.

your turn on your inside edge. It is mostly used to start a boat turning before you switch to one of the previous three maneuvers to complete your turn. It is also an intuitive and necessary turn that most of you mastered by necessity while riding a bicycle long before you bought your first slalom boat.

Now I think back to that same upstream I saw Fox doing. Looking at it this way that upstream, while still incredible, did not seem so impossible. Thinking back I can see him sliding the boat around as he approached the upstream gate so that he had angle back behind the gate. Then I can remember him dropping an edge so that the boat quit sliding and propelled itself behind the gate. Finally, he banked the boat as he hit the quick eddy water and, once the turn had started, dropped a small pivot to snap the boat around and head back towards the next gate. Fox had simply combined these four turns to make a hard turn easy.

**BANKING TURN**
Olympic Bronze and Silver medallist Dana Chladek. Photo by Chris Smith.

I know this all sounds tremendously intricate and difficult, but it really is easier than it sounds. The key to mastering these turns is to realize that, although each one has its own particular strokes and edges, they all have the same body posture and shoulder rotation. Keep these ideas in mind as you work on your strokes:

**Rotate About Your Spine:** You want to use your whole body to force the boat to turn. This means rotating from the very base of your spine. Truly using your whole back to rotate means that, from the base of your spine upwards, both sides of your body twist. One side will twist forward and one side will turn back.

**Aim Your Shoulders At Your Destination:** Get in the habit of facing your objective with your face and shoulders. I always try to think of my two shoulder-balls as headlights that I shine on my destination BEFORE I BEGIN MY TURN. By doing this you are better able to control the boat, better able to recruit all your torso muscles into helping you turn, and also you will finish your turn prepared to begin your next turn. I have countless memories of competitors who have aced a certain move yet left their shoulders behind the turn. Most often this catches up with them and they lose the race trying to get their shoulders orientated back in a direction where they can use them. Keep in mind the racquetball example. A good racquetball player always returns to the middle of the court after striking the ball. This way they are always ready to return the next ball regardless of where it goes. Be the same way with your strokes, always finish each stroke with your shoulders square on your destination and ready for the next stroke.

**Get Good Extension:** If you want the boat to turn, your strokes must get away from the boat. Most coaches will tell you to reach as far as you can go to get more leverage on the water. Keep in mind though that the more leverage you get on your strokes the more leverage your strokes get on you. Your strokes will only be powerful if you can use your entire torso to help push on the paddle so extend as far as you can while still rotating about your spine.

## Forward Sweeps

Sweeps are almost the perfect control stroke. Done correctly they are a powerful stroke that will cause the boat to turn and accelerate forward at the same time. These are the backbone of all your turns as draws and backstrokes are best used in combination with forward sweeps before and after them. In fact, almost every turn you make on slalom course will start with a sweep. If you don't believe how important a perfect sweep is watch a World Cup race sometime: you'll find the only thing that every top five racer has in common are fantastic sweeps.

The way you use your body on a good forward sweep is virtually identical to the way you use your body on a good forward stroke. Like a forward stroke it is powerful only if you are using your entire torso, shoulders and arms. Again, the effort must be

**FORWARD SWEEP**
At the start of a sweep, your eyes, shoulder and torso are should face your destination. Photo by Chris Smith.

coordinated such that each muscle involved in the stroke fires at the same time. Keep in mind that your spine is the center of this turn. This stroke rotates around the spine, meaning that the stroke side of your body will twist downstream while the opposite side will twist upstream. A common mistake many paddlers make is that they rotate only the stroke side of their body while leaving the rest of the body still. Here are some things to keep in mind: many of them are the same as a forward stroke:

**Sit up straight:** The lower vertebrate of your back need to be straight to rotate properly. This means that your lower back must be supported so that you can sit up. It can help to have a straight-backed seat and to consciously focus on sitting up straight.

**Rotate from the bottom of your torso:** Try and feel your one hip going forward and your other twisting back. It is easy to feel like you are using your back when in fact you are really only rotating your shoulders. Your whole back should twist and untwist at the same rate.

**Reach:** A sweep must get out and away from the boat in order to force the boat to turn. This is especially important at the start of the stroke. Without leaning forward extend your arms and rotate your torso (in to the turn), such that your blade is extend-

ed as far as possible towards the bow. Then as you execute the stroke be sure the blade describes a wide arc out and away from the boat.

**Keep your elbows in:** You need to tuck your elbows in and keep your top hand low. This keeps the stroke horizontal and allows the stroking blade to sweep out its widest arc. As you execute the sweeping stroke with your torso, simultaneously punch out with your top hand

**Plan the path of your paddle:** Many paddlers learn to use stern draws in lieu of forward sweeps when they learn to paddle. A stern draw is a stroke that simply pulls the stern to one side or the other but a sweep stroke starts near the bow and launches the boat forward as it turns. Master both of these strokes and learn when to use which.

## Advanced

Anyone can spin the boat on a sweep. Start to play with how much the boat goes forward with each stroke. Learn to dig your edge so that a sweep launches you forward as the boat spins. Next, practice slicing your edge into the water so that the bow pivots up into the air. Follow this slicing by a leveling of the boat so that the boat continues to spin on its tail once the stroke has been removed. Contrast these two reactions with sweeps done while the boat is flat and the edges are neutral. See how the boat slides around without either pivoting or carving itself forward. These "flatspins" should spin the boat in one place without really moving the boat in any particular direction.

## Elite

The sweep stroke that you use should be tailored to fit how you want the boat to turn. Carving sweeps should push the bow and come out at the hip, sliding sweeps should pull the stern sideways, and pivoting sweeps should shove the stern under the water.

Now that you've got your edges and strokes mastered it's time to start tweaking your strokes so that

**PIVOTING SWEEP**
A pivoting sweep is often used to lift the bow over rough water. Photo by Chris Smith.

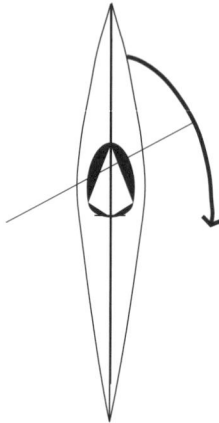

**CAVING SWEEP**
Use your outside edge as a skeg on a carving sweep to force the boat to move forward through a turn. Photo by Chris Smith.

**Carving Sweep**

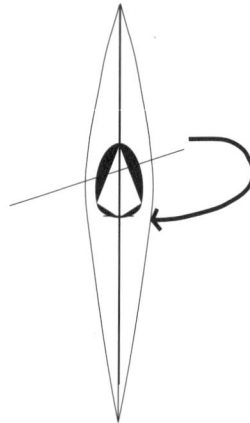

**Sliding Sweep**

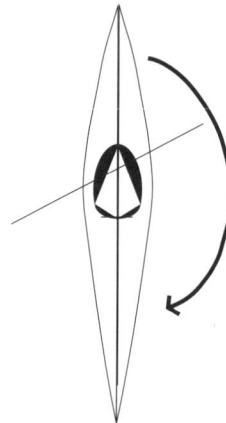

**Pivoting Sweep**

you get the best-desired response from your boat. Remember how we discussed earlier the four ways to turn your boat? Now we're going to shape our strokes so that, combined with our fantastic edge control, we have the ultimate in boat control. Head out to the flatwater with these tips and see if you can sweep your boat around in either a pivoting, carving or sliding turn!

**Pivot:** The sweep for the pivot turn probably most resembles the classic sweep you've been practicing. This sweep starts up by the bow and the initial part of the stroke is used to turn the boat 30-40 degrees. As the blade is beginning to come even with the paddler drop your edge and sit back just a hair. This is the part where the stern slices underwater and your bow will begin to rise. As you begin to run out of stroke, level the boat out with your hips so that it is slicing evenly through the water. You must be sure to level the boat after each stroke; otherwise the buoyancy of your boat will unwind you as soon as you take the blade out of the water for the next stroke.

**Carving:** Think of what your blade is doing to the boat. The first half of the stroke, the part between when you insert the blade at the bow and pull it to even with your hip, pushes the bow around the turn. The second half of the stroke, starting when the blade is even with your body until it reaches your boat back by the stern, pulls and slides the stern out! Remember that carving is just the opposite of sliding; in carving you do not want the stern to slide out. A carving sweep is just that first half of a sweep, starting from the bow and finishing when it comes even with the paddler. Work on using this stroke as the boat is moving. Try combining it with a radical outside-of-the-turn edge that will make the boat carve a firm arc around your turn.

**Sliding:** A sliding turn is just the opposite of this carving turn. You actually want the boat to skitter out and you do this by pulling the stern loose so that it has no grip and fishtails around the turn. This stroke is done by putting the sweep in about even with the hip, but as far out as you can reach, and then pulling from there towards your hip. The big problem you'll notice here is that it is almost impossible to maintain a good (focused on your destination) shoulder line while pulling the blade around towards your stern. The only way to get around this is to make this a stroke done almost entirely with your arms. Leave your shoulders focused on your destination and pull the stroke in TO JUST BEHIND YOUR HIP using mostly your arms instead of your torso.

## Back Sweeps

Like the forward stroke and forward sweep, the backstroke and back sweep are extremely similar. Unlike the forward strokes though, a pure backstroke is fairly uncommon on a slalom course. It is very rare that you'll find that you need, or can use, a series of backstrokes to go backward the way you use a series of forward strokes to go forward. For one thing it is seldom faster to paddle backwards for more than just a few strokes. For another, back paddling is difficult and more often requires back sweeps to effectively control the boat. Since this makes the back sweep so much more important than a back stroke using the back sweep as a model for your backstrokes works quite well.

The back sweep can be the most powerful and effective way to turn the boat. Almost all of us have been taught at one time or another to try and eliminate all the backstrokes out of our technique. Coaches often scorn this stroke thinking that it slows the boat too much and that it is an un-aggressive way to control the boat. The truth is that this stroke, like every other stroke, is well suited to some maneuvers and poorly suited to others. Often it is a fantastic way to slow the boat down while preparing for a difficult move or a great way to spin the boat quickly for hard-to-make turns. In many ways these coaches are correct though. This stroke, almost more than any other stroke, must be done correctly or your boat will stop dead in the water. Try and do your back sweeps like this:

### TRY THIS DRILL

There are countless drills to do for working your forward sweeps. The one I like best is to alternate between these different sweeps, three to side before switching to the other side. The idea here is that the boat is moving, serpentine-like across the lake.

Start the boat moving by paddling across the lake.

Now throw in a carving sweep to push the bow off to the side, be sure to rotate your body before you put the sweep in.

Follow that with a pivoting sweep. Sink the stern down below the surface and then lift your edge enough so that the boat continues to spin after the stroke comes out.

Finally put in a sliding sweep. Lean a little forward as you pull your stern to the side while lifting up the attacking edge. The boat should be sitting on the surface for this stroke with the stern skittering across the top of the water.

Now switch to the other side and repeat these three strokes. Do this in sets of seven per side.

**SLIDING SWEEP**
Scott Shipley using a sliding sweep to force the boat to exit tightly around an upstream during the Ocoee World Cup race. Photo by Chris Smith.

**Rotate from the torso:** Back sweeps are no different than any other turning stroke. Remember to turn from the very bottom of your torso. Again, BOTH of your shoulders should be focused towards the place you are turning. Remember to keep your turn centered around the base of your spine and avoid leaning out over the paddle for extension.

**Focus your eyes on where you are going:** Most often, despite your set-up, your boat will head towards where you are looking. Focus your attention on your destination. This means that as you finish your turn your shoulders should be already focused on where you are going. If you finish your back sweep and then have to straighten out your shoulders then you have not turned your shoulders enough at the start.

**Extend your paddle:** When working on your backstroke be sure to put the blade in the water all the

**BACK SWEEP SET-UP**
Scottie Mann using his whole upper body to set up a back sweep. Photo by Chris Smith.

way back at the stern! Your paddle-shaft should be parallel with your boat and both your hands should be on the inside of the turn. As you execute the stroke your blade should push out from the stern and then make a wide arc away from the boat.

**Keep your paddle horizontal:** Your paddle shaft should be as flat to the water as possible without losing grip from your blade. To do this you must keep your top hand low to the water as you execute the stroke.

### Advanced

As you practice your back sweeps work on how much you need to pivot for the quickest turn. Try everything from a flat spin, with the stern on a sliding across the water to a deep pivot with the bow as high as you can get it. Once you have found the ideal angle—the angle where the boat turns the quickest—then try and hold this exact height for an entire 360-degree spin. Jon Lugbil and Davey Hearn used to have pivot contests

**BOAT ON END**
Ethan Winger stands the boat on end with a powerful back sweep.
Photo by Peter Kennedy

when they were kids and still experimenting with these sorts of turns. They would choose a pole, either in flatwater or whitewater and pivot their bow up to whack each successive stripe on the gate. The winner was the paddler who had reached the highest stripe.

### Elite

Backstroke turns are no different than any other and you haven't truly mastered them until you can carve, slide and pivot the boat separately with these strokes. The trick to mastering these turns is to realize where to use them and why. There are three real advantages to using backstrokes to turn the boat. The first and most obvious reason is that they are the most powerful way to turn the boat. For this reason they are also the easiest way to control the boat and place it right where you want it. The third and most subtle reason is that these strokes can often be used to replace draws in places where you want to SLOW the boat down in preparation for a difficult move.

**TRY THIS DRILL:**

**The 360-degree spin test**

The 360-degree spin test is a fantastic way to test whether or not you have become proficient at turning your boat. The 360-degree spin test sounds amazingly simple, but you will only really be good at it if you have mastered all the concepts of good back sweeps and forward sweeps (i.e. extension, shoulder rotation, stroke path, etc.). It works like this: simply paddle at a medium pace across flatwater. At any time you choose throw in a forward sweep, back sweep, and forward sweep combination to pivot the boat in a circle. Remember, it is cheating if you use a draw at any point during the turn. If you can spin the boat a full 360 degrees and keep paddling with just these three strokes you have your turning strokes just about figured out. If not, check for these things:

Are you rushed? If you are having to rush from stroke-to- stroke as opposed to a controlled transition from stroke-to-stroke it is probably because you are unstable and need to work on your edge control.

Are you not finishing your turn? If you are having trouble finishing your turn it is most likely because you did not prepare your shoulders before EACH stroke. You must turn your shoulders before you start your forward sweep, then you must turn your shoulders again before you do your back sweep, then you must reset your shoulders again before you do your final forward stroke. A good goal to shoot for on this drill is 90 degrees of turn on the first forward sweep, followed by 180 degrees of turn on your back sweep, followed by the last 90 degrees on the last forward sweep. This means that you must rotate.

The carving turn with a back sweep generally takes the form of a stern rudder. Most often you would use this stroke to guide the boat through a dive gate (a downstream gate in an eddy) before dropping an edge, hauling on your rudder stroke, and carving out of the eddy and back into the current. For the most part the shaft will sit parallel to the direction that the boat is traveling and the blade is only arced out a few degrees to effect a turn. Essentially your blade is just a deep rudder in the water and has almost no resistance to the boat's forward momentum! While the blade work seems subtle, the rest of the turning rules still apply: You must turn your shoulders towards your destination, you must rotate from your spine and you still need good extension to make this an effective turn.

The sliding turn can take many forms but is primarily used in one of two ways. Quite often you will find that you need to do a reverse gate in an eddy. If you pivot this gate you will find that you have completed your turn without actually passing downstream through the gate, an awkward position at best. However if you enter the eddy headed downstream and slide the boat through the gate as you turn then you will skitter down through the gate at the same time you are turning to exit. The back sweep sliding turn is also often used to push back into a gate in the case that it is not worth the effort of paddling over to run the gate directly. These mini-backferries can be forced by the gates or simply be done to avoid having to skirt/jump whatever obstacle the gate is hidden behind. This stroke is done with a flat boat (loose stern) and is started by pushing the stern straight sideways with the first part of a stern sweep. The second, or middle third of the sweep is done with the blade fully extended and pushing straight back from the direction the boat is pointing. This part of the stroke causes the boat to both push back and spin at the same time. I usually finish the stroke with a draw if I want to finish the spin or else a sharp forward stroke if, as in the case of a back ferry, I want to launch the boat out of the turn.

The pivot turn is really the realm of the back sweep. Be sure to rotate so that you are completely facing your destination before you drop the stroke into the water. Then dig the edge quite aggressively as you begin your turn. As you finish the first third of your pivot flatten your edges and give the leading edge a slight angle towards the surface. For the remainder of the stroke the buoyancy of the stern will help you spin as much as your stroke does. These big back sweep pivots should be reserved for big turns or turns in which you must fight the current as the boat will stop while you are pivoting. Your turn will also be slow if you sink the stern too much and stall so just give it enough angle to get the bow out of the water and then begin to whip the turn around.

## Draws

Draw strokes are the _hot rod_ turning strokes of slalom. They are quick and powerful and fill the gap between turns you can do with forward sweeps and turns you must do on back sweeps. Done correctly a draw stroke can not only turn the boat almost as well as a backstroke, but also can accelerate the boat a little like a forward sweep. This stroke gives fantastic control and precision as the paddler has complete control over how much, and how fast, the boat turns. However this stroke does have its down sides. It does not propel the boat along as well as a forward sweep. In fact, unlike the other turning strokes, the draw is not a stand-alone stroke. Draws are usually ineffectual unless they are led by a forward or back sweep. They are the backbone of almost every turn in a slalom course and need to be mastered to get good at this sport.

I can't emphasize enough that draw strokes, like all turning strokes, follow the same few guidelines to be powerful and efficient. You rotate from your torso so

that you are focused on your objective, you must extend comfortably far from your center of rotation, and you must recruit and synchronize as much of the muscles in your torso, shoulders and arms all at once, as you can. Here is a step-by-step guide to doing your draw strokes:

**Pick your objective:** The worst sorts of draw strokes are done with your head facing straight forward. Paddlers in this situation simply apply a force and wait until they feel they are turned enough. Decide how far you want to rotate your boat before you put the draw stroke in the water and then focus your eyes and shoulders on that objective. Let the boat rotate beneath you until your entire body is focused on your objective.

**Rotate your body from the torso:** Again, as you rotate your shoulders to put the blade in the water, rotate from down low. Your body should be twisted from the torso up through to your neck.

**GLIDING DIVE GATE RUDDER**
The stern rudder can be used to carve the boat through a difficult maneuver without sacrificing boat speed. Photo by Chris Smith.

**GOOD DRAW STROKE**
Place the paddle outside of your objective on a draw stroke. Your arms and paddle should frame the view of your destination. Photo by Chris Smith.

**Focus your shoulders on your objective:** In practice, on flatwater, I usually pick something about 110 degrees of turn around. Then I turn from the torso until my entire shoulder line is facing my objective. The mistake people most often make when working on this sort of rotation is that they rotate their outside shoulder forward, but leave their inside shoulder facing straight ahead. Make sure that your outside-of-the-turn shoulder rotates forward and your inside shoulder rotates back. Everything should rotate about the spine.

**Place the paddle outside of your objective:** Your paddle must be put in the water far enough around that you can finish your turn before you run out of stroke. Create an imaginary line that is your line of sight between your eyes and your destination. If your stroke goes inside this line, which is to say between the line of sight and your bow, you will run out of stroke before you finish turning the boat. If you put this stroke outside the line of sight, meaning that your line of sight to your destination is between your bow and where you put the stroke in the water, then your bow can face the destination while your stroke is still in the water. Sound complicated? An easier way to think about it is that you must look under your paddle shaft at your objective. If you are looking over your shaft you will not have enough stroke, if you are looking through the loop made by your arms and the paddle then you are in good shape.

**Think about turning your boat:** The most common focus for a paddler is to pull the paddle towards the boat. It seems like a small difference, but you should focus on pulling your knees, and thus boat, even with your shoulders. A good draw turn follows this sequence, turn your body first, put the blade in the water for grip, now turn the boat even to your original shoulder line. If done correctly you will finish the stroke with your shoulders facing straight ahead, relative to the boat, and also directly facing your objective.

### Advanced

By the time you have reached an advanced level you should be very proficient at turning the boat with draws. Now you need to learn to do your draws so that the boat not only makes a quick turn, but rockets out of that turn with some forward speed. A good example of this is when a boat makes a quick turn in the pocket of an upstream (see the section on upstreams for a description of the "pocket"). If the draw was used to simply turn the boat then the paddler is left dead in the back of the upstream gate. If the draw is done so that it not only snaps the boat around in the pocket of the turn but also accelerates from there towards the eddy line then you will have saved an entire stroke and more than a second in exiting the gate.

The method for nursing forward speed out of a turning stroke is intricate and takes a lot of time to learn. Using your edges and turning strokes to carry speed requires a balance of body, boat, and blade position. On flatwater the turn is done like this (you'll have to fill in all the basics from above):

* Paddle at a medium pace across a lake before beginning the turn with a forward sweep stroke on the outside of the turn. This sets up the draw stroke by giving the boat speed and initiating the turn.
* Drop your outside edge abruptly and sharply as you rotate your body and place the stroke. Your body should be upright or sitting back just a hair at this point. This should begin a quick deep descent of your stern below the surface.
* Continue to dive the stern for the first part of the draw stroke. As it reaches a good turning depth (about 6-12 inches below the surface) flatten out the stern so that it has just a slight canter towards coming back to the surface. This way the boat buoyancy is now helping to turn the boat.
* As your draw and your boat run into their last third of turn sit forward with the stroke. As you sit forward flatten out the boat. This combination of body, boat, and blade position should shoot you out of your turn like a pea in a shooter.

### Elite

An elite level draw turn, like all turns, needs to be broken down into pivoting, carving, and sliding turns. Draw turns, much more than the usually abrupt sweep strokes, tend to transition from one type of turn to another. In other words a draw can often start out as a carving turn and then slide the stern out before dropping the pivot stroke. Separate each of these turns now so that you can master each type of turn before you try and mush them all together into an upstream gate.

### TRY THIS DRILL:

First try spinning the boat around and around on a back sweep pivot turn. This is a fantastic drill both for working on your backstrokes and working on your pivots/edge control. Alternate between seeing how high you can lift your bow and how long you can spin around while holding your bow at exactly the same height. You should find that it is actually easier to lift your bow way up in the air than it is to steadily hold it just a little bit off of the water.

Another great drill is to hang a single striped slalom pole. Then paddle past the pole with a little speed. When you are just under half a boat length past the pole throw in a back sweep and pivot the boat 180 degrees. As your bow comes around slice the stern so that you tick the gate on the lowest stripe.

Now do the same drill again only this time hit the second stripe. See how many stripes you can climb to in a row. If you miss a stripe then force yourself to start over. To make the drill especially hard, put the pole on an eddy line and start the pivot turns as you go into the current.

**Pivoting turn:** Unlike the sweeps, almost every draw stroke pulls the bow around as much as it pushes the stern in. For the most part the pivot part of the pivot turn is done with the hips and edges. The turn should be started with a sweep to begin turning the boat, and then the stern edge is dug in immediately as the draw is executed. Often, if the current can be used to help, this is easy and the draw can be fairly subtle. These draws are usually towards the bow and are mostly a lateral pull towards the boat from in front of the boat's pivot point. In extreme cases, as when you are doing large turns in flatwater, the stern must be sunk entirely with energy from the draw stroke. In this case the stroke is extended quite far back so that the first part of your draw actually works a bit as a backstroke (the blade is open faced with the power face facing forward towards the bow), this serves to sink the stern and begin the pivot.

**Carving turn:** The carving turn opens a whole new can of worms when done with a draw. They are best done with a whole new stroke, one most of us don't learn until we are at an elite level in this sport. In America the stroke was taught to us from a French coach who, at the time, spoke poor English. The Americans initially misunderstood the stroke and named it the "C" stroke for the path they thought the blade should travel through the water. The British, who knew the stroke all along, call it a bow rudder, which seems to make a lot more sense once you get the stroke figured out. Here's the best, although round about, way to explain this stroke:

Scull your boat sideways across a lake. Do this by extending your paddle out to the side and moving the blade back and forth through the water with the blade face open towards the direction the blade is traveling. Most of us learned to scull the boat sideways back and forth across a lake on our first few outings in a boat. Now only scull the blade forward. This is the basis of the stroke, it is a forward scull with the bottom hand moving forward and your top hand moving back so that the blade slices FORWARD

**PIVOTING DRAW**
The pivoting draw can quickly snap the boat around a sharp turn. Photo by Chris Smith.

**THE "C-STROKE"**
The blade is inserted out to the side and skulled forward as the boat negotiates a turn. Photo by Chris Smith.

The sliding draw is often used to set up a tight approach upstream. Note that in the first photo the sliding draw is used with the edge free to start the boat spinning without tightening the approach. In the second frame a sliding sweep is used for the same reason. Only once the boat is behind the gate are the edges used to grip the water.
Photo by Chris Smith.

through the water. Now instead of doing this skulling out to the side of your boat do it at a 45 degree angle in front of you. If you lead with a forward sweep on the outside of your turn and then rotate your shoulders and drop your outside edge while you are doing the bow rudder stroke, then you should have a carving draw that rockets the boat forward through the water. This stroke should initially feel quite odd because you are pushing the blade forward through the water while it is accelerating the boat forward through the turn. This is similar to skating on ice skates. When ice-skating you are pushing off of an ice skate that is moving forward to push your body forward faster.

**Sliding turn:** Sliding draw turns are about as much fun as trying to paddle in molasses. Still they are often necessary. The idea to keep in mind is that a sliding turn is used to turn the boat without moving the boat in the direction of turn. These sliding draw turns are often used to turn the boat in water too powerful to risk a pivot or else to get the proper entry trajectory into tight approach upstreams (we'll get more into this later). Most often this is done by using the draw as an opened faced backstroke far out to the side. The boat is usually left flat with neutral edges so that the stern skitters across the top of the water as the boat is spun around. Typically, at the start of the stroke, the blade face is opened enough that the stroke can simply be pulled on, if need be, at the end of the draw.

## Upstreams

The racer is a mask of pain as he sprints below Callahan's Ledge on Tennessee's Ocoee River towards Humongous. Suddenly the look disappears as he approaches the churning eddy behind the wave guarding the entrance. He is all grace now as he effortlessly slices his bow behind the gate and lets his stern follow. With one quick stroke he is back in the current and headed across to the final gates of the course.

For much of the crowd, who knows nothing of slalom racing, he seems to be paddling a hair better than the rest. To those who have tried it, his two-stroke upstream is nothing short of a miracle. Slalom racers spend long hours trying to perfect the "two-stroke upstream." Depending on the course, upstreams can come in many shapes and forms. There can be upstreams in almost any location in any eddy and, should the designer be feeling demonic enough, they can even be found in midstream currents. The technique for getting through them fast and efficiently stems from mastering the basic flatwater eddy turn.

There are three parts to a good upstream gate, the approach, the turn, and the exit. The key to acing a gate is to analyze the gate in the opposite order you will negotiate it. Since the most important part of a fast upstream gate is a fast exit, it makes sense that you would start from the ideal exit and work backwards. When I look at any upstream gate, especially at big races, I think first of how to get out of the gate. The French maintain that the first rule of slalom is, "Never go away from the finish line." To follow this rule, look for a way to exit the upstream gate

## TRY THIS DRILL: Snake on the Lake

There are a ton of drills you can do that use the draw. The simplest of which is to simply do the draws, round and round, in a circle. This is a good way to focus on the mechanics of the stroke. However, since it works at such low speeds and does not combine with other strokes it doesn't seem to me to be the best way to get the feel for good draw strokes. Here are a couple of drills I like because they keep the boat moving across the lake and feel much more similar to a draw done on a slalom course:

**Tight Snake Drill:** The objective of this drill is to combine a sharp pivoting sweep with a pivoting draw. They are simply done one after the other like this:

* Paddle at a medium pace across the lake
* Turn your shoulders to the left and do a carving sweep on your right side.
* Now, return your shoulders to the left and do a sharp pivoting draw on your left side.
* As you run out of play in this draw stroke turn your shoulders back towards the right side and flip your blade around to set up a left side sweep.
* Sharply execute the left side sweep so that your edge digs, as in a pivoting sweep. The boat should do a sharp reversal in the direction that it is spinning.
* As you run out of play on that stroke flatten your boat so that you are stable on your pivot turn as you return your shoulders and snap a draw stroke on your right side.
* Again, as your draw runs out return your shoulders to the left and set up a right side pivoting sweep.

You can see how the cycle repeats, right draw left sweep, left draw right sweep. This is an aggressive drill—strokes are executed sharply and with extreme power. I usually do these in sets of seven to a side.

**Wide snaking drill:** This drill is elegant and smooth where the tight snake drill was sharp and abrupt. The objective of this drill is to work on carving wider turns that you can paddle through. The wide snaking drill is done by combining carving draws with carving sweeps as you zig-zag across the lake. You are going to use two sweep and two draws for each direction of turn. The idea is that you are not forcing the boat around a turn, but simply giving it an impulse to turn with a c-stroke on the inside of the turn, then paddling with a carving sweep/forward stroke on the outside of the turn, then giving it another impulse on the c-stroke on the inside of the turn. Your boat will loop around about 180 degrees for each combination of two sweeps and two C's. However, on each C-stroke you will have only turned the boat about 60 degrees. The rest of the turn is accomplished with the spin momentum left over from these two strokes.

* Paddle at a medium pace across the lake.
* Turn your shoulders to the left and do a carving sweep on your right side.
* Now return your shoulders to the left and do a c-stroke. Your boat should be turned 90 degrees away from the direction you were originally heading.
* Now turn your shoulders to the right and push a carving sweep on your left to reverse the direction of spin.
* Again, return your shoulders to the right and do a c-stroke that turns you about 60 degrees.
* Return your shoulders and do a carving sweep on the left.
* Return your shoulders and do another c-stroke that brings you around perpendicular to the direction you were originally traveling, but now headed towards the right.
* Repeat this same combination, snaking from side to side for as long as you want. Be sure that you are smooth and concise on each stroke. Try not to be rushed or overly powerful.

**TIGHT EXIT HERE**
Never go away from the finish line! Margaret Langford exiting tightly around an upstream gate. Photo by Peter Kennedy.

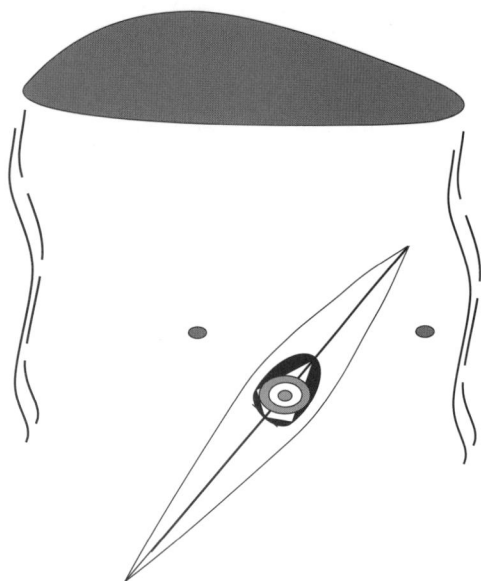

when the upstream is not in flatwater.

The middle phase of executing an upstream gate is simply the turn done at the _spot_. If you have selected the right _spot_, and you have had a proper approach, this is the easiest part of the turn. Your objective in the turn should be the same as it was in working on basic draw strokes. You need to turn at the torso and focus your head and shoulders on your exit trajectory  From this position it should be easy to execute a powerful and concise draw that turns your boat crisply towards this exit trajectory.

Now that you know how to find, and turn at, the "spot," go upstream and look down on the gate as you would in a real race. The "spot" is behind and below the gate and the most direct way of getting there is blocked by the gate-line. Don't be alarmed. You need to find out how to get from upstream of the gate to back behind the gate, arriving with the correct angle and trajectory. This is the approach, the initial phase of an upstream. Getting your approach right is the most important part of an upstream gate. If you can't accurately shove your boat onto the "spot," you won't get out of the gate in one quick burst and your shot at a medal will be lost.

The trick is to not let yourself be drawn too closely into the turn. Upstreams, much like corners in an auto race, tend to suck the racer in so close that he or she has to slow down to negotiate the turn. Don't let it suck you in! Before you try an approach paddle downstream past the gate, keeping about three-quarters of a boat length away from the gate. As you go past the gate, look over at the spot.  When you can see the spot without looking through the gate, then you can see your approach.

The idea is to paddle the boat straight downstream and slowly meld the boat's trajectory into your desired line. By the time your bow starts to poke into the eddy, past the inside pole, you should already be turned sideways. Try to take one last powerful sweep stroke as you leave the current and begin your glide towards the "spot." This is called the entry sweep and it will do two things: it will give the boat lateral momentum; and it will start the boat on a turn that will shoot it out of the gate. Top racers usually have their boats parallel to the gate-line before they get downstream of the gate. Remember that when you arrive at the "spot" you want to be facing out of the gate! And that means practice. Keep the approach separate from the exit and focus on landing on that spot again and again. Each time you get there face out of the gate towards the current.

Now take a look at the upstream gate from front to back, stroke by stroke:

**The Approach:** The key to saving time in an upstream is really in exiting fast, not in going in fast. Focus on control during your approach and save your explosive power for the exit.  Your approach trajectory should be wide enough away from the gate that you have room to turn and come in at the gate from the side.  In general I try and imagine a line heading upstream from the inside pole at a 45 degree angle to the gate line.  You should at least be below this 45

and start heading for the finish line while traveling upstream as little as possible. The less time you spend in the eddy the better. To do this I look for a place in the eddy that I call, "the spot," it's the one place where, with a well-placed exit sweep stroke, I can push the boat back into the current and towards my objective. Try and find this spot in flatwater. When coaching, I often have athletes play a simple game to find this _spot_. I have them go to the gate, sit just downstream of the line between the poles (the so-called "gate-line") and then try to paddle out of the gate with a single stroke.  The objective of this game is to find the place where, with one well-executed stroke, they shoot out of the gate and into the current headed downstream.  On flatwater this spot is just downstream of the gate line with your boat pointing at about 45 degrees up and out of the gate. You should be a full arm_s length away from the inside pole.  Keep in mind that the spot is different

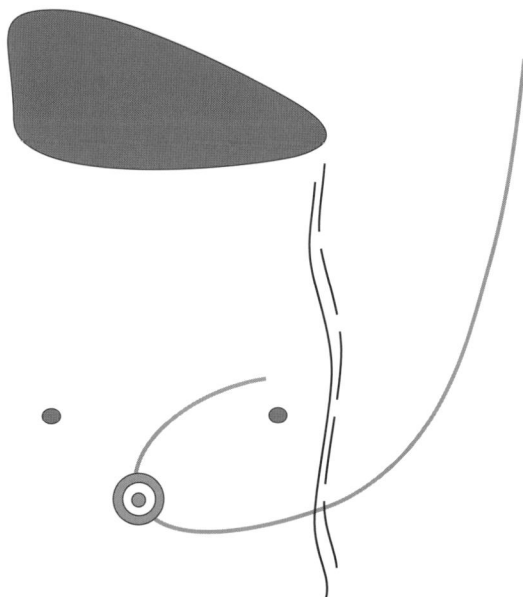

to make your approach.

You must get behind the gate on your entry in order to exit the gate quickly. To do that you need to convert the downstream momentum of your approach into lateral momentum towards the _spot_. A good test of this is if your boat is at least parallel to the gate line as you pass beneath the inside pole. There are several possible stroke combinations that do this. I prefer to actually do an extra sweep and draw out in the current. For those of you keeping track, this is one carving sweep and one carving draw to set up, and then one sweep of the appropriate kind to drive me in behind the gate and one very snappy draw to snap my turn at the spot.

You are on final approach once you have turned the boat and are aimed at, and heading towards, the spot. From this point you should have a clear shot at the gate. Take an aggressive sweep on the outside to shoot you into the gate. I tend to do this stroke earlier rather than later—to make sure that I_m not rushed—and fairly aggressively. This entry sweep, for me, feels the same way I feel when I launch the boat off of a ledge with a sweep-in short, I try and throw the boat in behind the gate so that it will land in the right spot with the right angle

**The Turn:** The same shoulder rotation that was so important in the basic strokes is key in executing good upstream gates. By the time you reach the spot you should already have your head and shoulders focused on the exit. This is why I tend to do my entry sweep a little earlier than most paddlers. After you launch yourself towards the spot, let the boat glide as you rotate your torso so that your head and shoulders are facing out of the gate in the direction you_d like to head. From this point relax a little because you_ve got a lot of good things going for you. First off, your body is already turned ahead of your boat so your boat is beginning an effortless natural arc in the proper direction. Secondly, because of the inevitable pressure on your outside edge, also due to your body position, the water is going to help you turn the boat. Let the water do as much of the work as you can! Here is a key element to a successful turn: you must quit focusing on the "spot" after your entry sweep. You are now focusing on your exit, you should be looking at your exit line waiting for the boat to slide into the gate far enough that you can see where it is you_d like to go. You are waiting for what I call an _open door_. As soon as you can see out of the gate, snap your draw stroke so that your boat whips around and faces towards your exit trajectory. One note here; finish this turn on your draw to the point where you are facing out of the gate at about 45 degrees to the gate line. Too often people give up on the draw stroke and drop their exit sweep earlier (too early). If this exit sweep is done while the boat is still arcing around behind the gate it will cause your edge to slide out and you will lose your run (momentum) out of the gate.

**The Exit:** The entry to an upstream is controlled, the turn is crisp and precise, but the exit, the exit is powerful and explosive. At this point you should have set up your exit angle with a precise draw that

**APPROACH TO GATE**
As you enter the upstream your boat should be at least parallel to the poles and your shoulders should be leading your turn. Photo by Chris Smith.

**TURN**
Once on the spot focus your upper body on the exit and snap the turn with a draw stroke. Photo by Chris Smith.

**EXIT**
Exit with a powerful sweep to reaccelerate the boat back into the current. Photo by Chris Smith.

has the boat pointed just so you can exit on a single stroke. Now reach through the gate-getting your paddle through the gate gives you extension and prevents your paddle from becoming tangled in the poles-and place an exit sweep firmly in the water. Now snap that stroke so that the boat launches out of the gate and ALONG YOUR PLANNED TRAJECTORY. If you are heading across the current, this should be more of a forward stroke, and if you are heading out of the gate and downstream, this should be more of a sweep. Immediately after exiting the gate re-

## TRY THIS DRILL:

### Breakin' down the Ups

As you have probably guessed by now I like to take everything step by step. The same is true of working on upstreams. Slalom is a game of setting yourself up for the next move. That makes your exit the most important part of your upstream because it is your exit that will launch you into your next move. It is for this reason that I master the exit first before going back and working on the approach and the turn. Try this drill for mastering upstreams:

**Find the Spot:** Just relax and sit in the gate. There is no need to jump right into doing your exits just yet. Get a feel for where you want to be in the gate. Sit just below the gate line and away from the inside pole enough that you can see your exit. The gate should be framing exactly the line that is the quickest path to the current. Before you do anything else close your eyes and visualize just the last part of your approach. You should be shooting laterally in behind the gate with your boat parallel to the gate line and your torso rotated so that your head and shoulders are facing out of the gate. Your draw stroke should be at the ready waiting for this one moment. Now open your eyes. The moment you are waiting for is the moment you can see exactly what you are looking at now...an open door. When you see this on your approach it is time to snap your draw and begin your exit.

**The Exit:** Now reach through the gate with your shoulders rotated for a good sweep stroke. You should have good extension and your shoulders should be focused on your exit. Snap that exit sweep with all your strength. The exit sweeps from upstream gates should consistently be the most

powerful strokes you take on a slalom course.

Do this again and again until you are exiting on one stroke with speed. By now you should be very familiar with exactly where the spot is in this gate.

**The Approach:** For now let's do a very simple approach. Remember the 45-degree line that angles up from the inside pole of the upstream you are doing. Approach the gate from above and about a boat length wide of the eddy (or the inside pole). Continue paddling straight downstream until you cross this imaginary 45-degree line. As you cross it begin to arc in towards the gate, from this point forward focus your head and shoulders on the spot. Your entire turn should take place below this 45-degree line. Now, as you come within a stroke and a half of the spot launch yourself with a powerful sweep on the outside. This sweep should be a carving sweep so that your shoulders can remain focused on the spot. At this point you are gliding behind the gate, rotate your torso and focus your shoulders on your exit. Now just let the boat glide deeper into the gate until the poles of the gate frame your exit towards the current.

Try this again and again. At first you should do this part of the drill without finishing your turn and exiting the gate. Get a real feel for the glide that runs you into the gate. Also get a real feel for how you can use the water, and your edges, to turn the boat without having to do all that work yourself. You can also try this drill without paddling once you've reached the gate. If the boat tends to glide up through the poles on its own they you have made a nice entry.

**The Turn:** The last part of this drill is easy. Simply add the snap of your draw that will link your entry to your exit. As easy as it sounds, many of us spend a large part of our racing careers mastering just these simple maneuvers. Once you think you've mastered the perfect up check for these things:

Do you have room for a good draw stroke or are you squeezed too tightly on the gate?

Do you have speed when you are exiting?

focus your shoulders on your next objective and follow your exit sweep with two or three more powerful acceleration strokes.

The basic flatwater upstream is really just one unique case of an upstream. In a race almost every upstream will be negotiated differently depending on what sort of water the gate is placed in and what sort of approach and exit are dictated by the course designer. Many racers like to treat each gate as a unique case. In training they would try and practice as many of these cases as possible with the hope that, in a race situation, they would have practiced something similar before. I look at it a little differently. I treat this flatwater upstream as my basis for comparison. After lots of practice I am extremely familiar with where I want to be in every part of this basic maneuver. Each time I look at an upstream on a race course or in training I adjust this flatwater upstream such that it works in that particular situation. Try this in your training and see if it helps to take apart difficult gate combinations so that they can be understood much more easily. Here are a couple of basic examples that you will see on a lot of race courses.

## The Tight Approach Upstream

**The Problem:** The problem with tight approach upstreams is that you are coming straight down on the gate. Given a chance you would have approached this gate much more from the side than you are able to do on this course. Ideally, by the time you reach the gate, you would like to have the boat turned parallel with the gate line, and heading back behind the gate. On a tight approach upstream you are lacking two important factors that would have helped make this a faster gate. The first factor is a trajectory that puts you behind the gate and the second is the boat angle necessary to pass beneath the gate-line with your boat angle at least parallel to the gate line. Keep in mind that, even though you have a tight approach, the _spot_ is still in the same place, it is still the best place from which to exit the gate. The question is how to best deal with such a difficult approach?

**The Approach:** The best way to get a good approach is often to _wiggle_ out a bit. This is a maneuver where, if you have enough room, you paddle out a bit from the gate so that you can approach on a more ideal trajectory. Depending on how much room you have this can mean paddling the boat in an arc so that it heads away from the upsteam before hooking back in behind it. Or a quick snapping sweep stroke that pushes the boat out while swinging the angle back towards the gate.

Your second option, if you cannot efficiently wiggle out is to get the angle without getting the trajectory. This is a very effective way to deal with tight approach upstreams, especially on canals. Remember that when we discussed the three different types of sweeps—carving, pivoting and sliding—that a sliding sweep was meant to turn a boat without pushing the boat in the direction of the turn. This is exactly what

**WIGGLE OUT APPROACH TO TIGHT UPS**
If a gate above the upstream forces a tight approach, the paddler can often "wiggle out" just after that gate to allow for a normal entry into the upstream. Photo by Chris Smith.

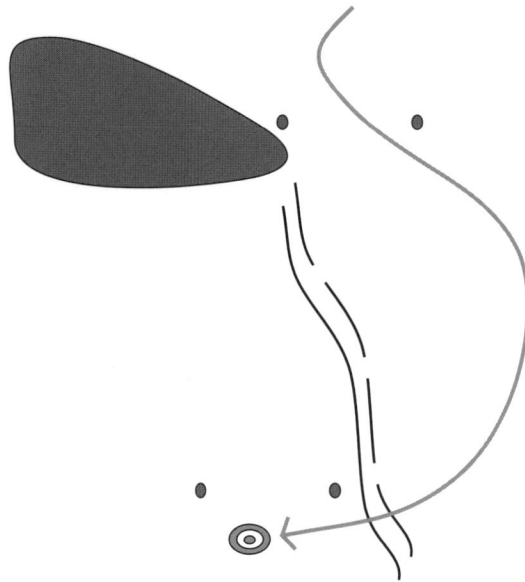

**UPTIGHT WIGGLE OUT**
Your approach to the gate should "bow" out and give you room to drive in to the spot.

you need when you must execute a tight approach upstream. If you do a bow sweep you will push the bow in, towards the gate, and make your approach even tighter. If you do a sliding sweep you will rotate your boat like a top around your center of rotation. This will give you the angle you need for your approach without having to travel along a lateral approach line. Unfortunately this does not give you the lateral momentum you need to get into the pocket so come into the gate much higher than normal.

**The Turn:** Ideally your turn will be the same as always. If you can effectively wiggle for a proper approach this is certainly the case. On the sliding approach you will often find that your boat does not end up driving itself deep enough behind the gate. In this case you will not get an ideal exit angle as the inside pole will block your exit. This is called getting _stuck on the pole," In this case turn the boat so that it faces as much out of the gate as possible.

**The Exit:** If you did reach the spot then, obviously, take the ideal exit. In the case that your exit is pinched because you were stuck on the pole (you didn't go deep enough to reach the "spot," then

**UPTIGHT SLIDE**
If there isn't room to wiggle then simply slide the stern around. This will give you the correct angle for the upstream but your entry will be a little short.

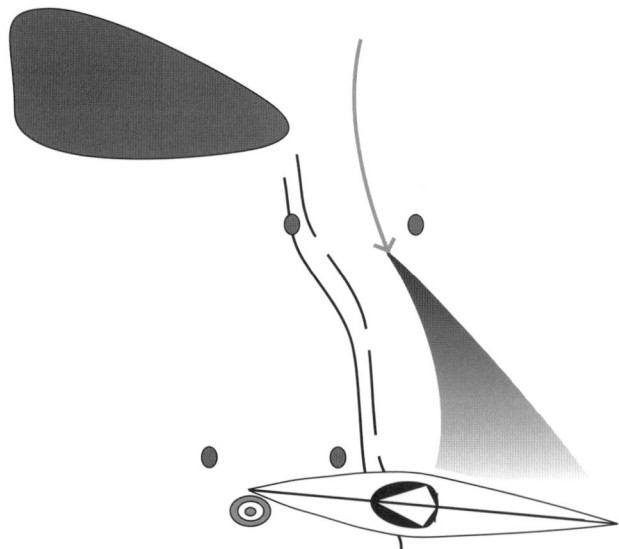

use a large powerful bow sweep to push yourself up and around the pole linked with a stern draw to get the boat headed downstream again as you get past the pole.

## Upstreams in the Current

**The Problem:** These are tough because in a typical upstream you are counting on the eddy to help you turn and to keep you from being swept downstream. Your turn and your exit angle are also quite different because, given that there is current through the gate itself, you must finish your turn facing directly upstream so that your boat doesn't get pushed out of the gate before you are ready to exit.

**The Approach:** The approach on an up in the current is essential. Since the gate is in the current there will be no eddy beneath your gate to kill your downstream momentum and to help you turn the boat. Worse still, if you wait until you get to the gate to do your turn you will find that, while you are busy cranking the boat around so that it faces upstream, the current will be pushing you further and further downstream. You must do this part ahead of time. An ideal approach to an upstream in the current is to set up a ferry into the gate. On your initial approach to the gate come in quite wide with a carving turn. This will convert your momentum from downstream momentum to cross current momentum. As you come into a final approach actually continue to turn your boat, so that you are ferry-carving into the gate from the side. The boat should come underneath the inside pole facing almost upstream with the outside edge firmly locked into the current.

**The Turn:** First off, the _spot_ for an up in the current is just inside the inside pole. If you were to go any deeper you would have to exit at an angle. If you do this you will be washed into the inside pole by the current as you try to exit. Secondly and for the same reason, your turn should be a carving turn that simply turns you back upstream again with just a little angle out of the gate.

**The Exit:** The exit from the gate will need to be a powerful combination of two strokes. The first part of your exit sweep will most likely be a carving sweep that pushes the boat up and out of the gate. That stroke should then be continued with a stern draw that turns the boat downstream again. Also important is that while you will be carving your edge for the first part of this sweep to rocket yourself up and out of the gate, you must flatten your stern (or pivot it) for the second part of the sweep so that the boat can turn downstream again.

## S-turns

**The Problem:** The difficult thing about s-turns is that the "spot" is determined by how you wish to exit. In a regular upstream this creates the challenge of needing to get back in behind the gate so that you can turn on the far side and make a quick exit back out the way you came in. For an S-gate the opposite is true, you will hit the "spot" in the early

**AN UP IN THE CURRENT**
Ferry the boat into an upstream in the current and stay tighter to the inside pole to prevent the current from sweeping you downstream. The exit stroke should quickly shoot you out of the gate. Photo by Chris Smith.

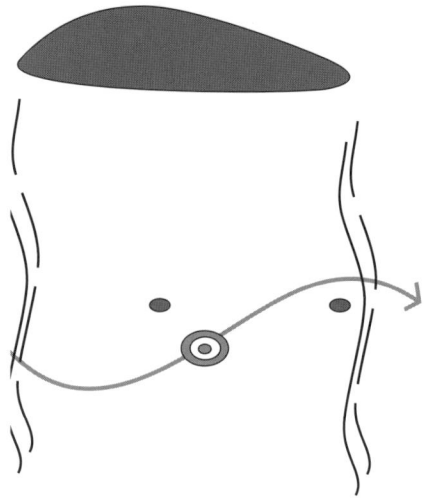

**AN S-TURN**
The exit on an S-turn should begin before you enter the gate. Photo by Chris Smith.

part of your approach to the gate. The true challenge in S-turns lies in being able to prepare enough in advance that you can be ready to exit as soon as you come within reach of the gate. Since this is a one shot deal, you've got to have the guts to really go for this one.

**The Approach:** The thing to keep in mind on an S-turn gate is that the _spot_ is in the same place. There is still only one spot from which you can exit on one stroke. This _spot_ is in the same place it would have been had you done a normal up, FROM THE OTHER SIDE! Think about it, the placement of your ideal exit is not related to your entry. For an S-turn gate you exit around the far pole, the same way you_d exit if you came in from the far side to do a regular upstream gate. Your approach, however, is quite different. Your inside pole is now opposite from the pole you will exit around. The _spot_ is just underneath that inside pole. To have a fast turn you must arrive at the _spot_ with the angle and trajectory you need to exit. This is to say that when you go beneath the inside pole line you MUST already be finished turning into the gate and begin turning out of the gate and you must also have stopped your downstream momentum. For a really fast gate try putting your exit stroke in before you even get to the gate!

**The Turn:** The turn, as I mentioned, is part of your approach. Turn your boat so that you are facing out of the gate before you go beneath the inside pole.

The Exit: The exit is the key to a fast S-turn. The trick to getting cleanly and quickly out of an S-turn is to nail that exit at the earliest possible moment. Your exit stroke should not only launch you through the gate, but turn you downstream at the same time. In fact, it is the downstream arc that makes the gate possible on one stroke. This is why it is so important to finish your turn into the gate before you get to it. From the moment you pass beneath the inside pole you must be turning the boat downstream. If you are not turned upstream enough to do this then you will have a slow and likely dirty exit.

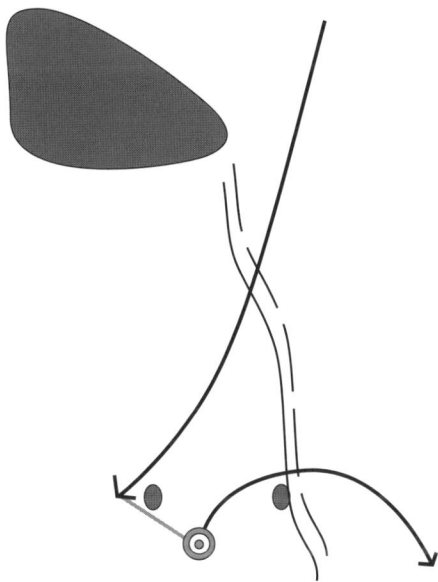

**A MERANO TURN**
The trick to a Merano gate is spinning the boat and pushing it backwards as you enter. This allows for a quick exit from the "spot." Photo by Chris Smith.

## Merano Turns

**The Problem:** A Merano turn is often used when a gate straddles a strong eddyline and the paddler would drop very low in the eddy while doing a conventional upstream. Instead the paddler can squeeze himself between the gate and shore and back down to the spot.

Merano turns are a problem in themselves. This is such a difficult maneuver that you will seldom find a place on a slalom course where it is consistently faster than a regular upstream. The move consists of coming into an upstream above the gate and then backing downstream past the gate on the opposite side of the poles. The problem inherent in this maneuver is that you are trying to wiggle, slide, and back-paddle directly onto a "spot" that sits in your blind-spot for most of the execution.

**The Approach:** There are a lot of different reasons to do a Merano and your approach is as much based on the situation as it is on anything else. Essentially the point of your approach in this type of gate is to put yourself in position for a quick exit, which is to say to put yourself on the _spot_ ready to exit. If your Merano gate is in an eddy or any situation where the water underneath the inside pole is not moving then you'll need to approach the gate more from above. This will give your boat the downstream momentum it needs to slide down below the gate while you turn, thus leaving you sitting on the spot. If, on the other hand, there is some current underneath the inside pole then you will need to approach more from the side, sweeping in just above the gate so that your downstream momentum is slowed sufficiently that you will not wash down below the gate while you are turning.

**The Turn:** The turn on a Merano is often extremely tricky. The reason why is that, depending on your approach, you will need to not only turn once you get below the gate, but also push your boat backwards towards the middle of the gate where the "spot" is. To do this most of us use a sort of com-

**A HIGH EXIT APPROACH**
The entry into an upstream can be adjusted to allow for quick high exits from the gate Photo by Chris Smith.

pound back-stroke. The first part of the stroke is more of a back-stroke to push the boat back a little while the second is a draw to finish the turn. In most cases you will need to open your shoulders quite a lot to complete this draw with the right boat angle. In the case of a flatwater eddy you_ll need·to finish our turn with the boat angled out of the gate at about a 45 degree angle (remember, the _spot_ is in the same place no matter how you approach the gate. It is the place, and boat angle, from which you can exit with a single stroke). In the case of a moving water gate you_ll want to have the boat facing more upstream so that you don_t get swept downstream into the outside pole by the current while you are exiting.

**The Exit:** The exit is the same as any other upstream. Remember that this part of the gate is crushingly powerful and crisp. Catapult yourself out of the gate!

## High-Exit Upstreams

**The Problem:** Most upstreams that you'll find in competition will not be textbook cases. In addition to having differing entries, as you might have with a tight-approach or an upstream in the current, there are often differing exits. Most gates are quicker when done with a tight exit but there are times when you need to carry up the eddy either to catch a particular wave or to get a better approach on a difficult move. Rather than pocketing the gate and then taking extra strokes up the eddy it is sometimes better to make your actual turn in the eddy higher. The strategy here is to carve into the eddy just below the inside pole and carry your turn up through the gate. The "spot" in this case is actually above the gate line!

**The Approach:** For this approach to work you must be coming at the gate from the side. The idea is that you are going to carve right up through the gate before you even begin your turn. Since you will have so much speed, it is paramount that you either

bank or carve this turn-a slide or a pivot will send you skittering into the outside pole. The approach is to charge right in as tight to the inside pole as you can. Your "spot" for this gate is just upstream and inside the outside pole. If this is a good eddy you should be carried up through the gate line as soon as you hit the eddy.

**The Turn:** Due to the fact that you are now completely above the gate you are able to convert your carve/bank entry into whatever turn is necessary. Generally a carve would be better if you want to carry further up the eddy or a pivot is a better option if you want to snap your turn and head for your next objective.

**The Exit:** Again, your exit is more dependant on why you chose this sort of up then it is to the gate itself. You do have the opportunity here though to tailor your exit to help make your next move easier. If you are heading across a wave get control of the boat's rotation before you leave the eddy, if you are headed towards a difficult offset give the boat some extra spin as you cross the eddyline.

## Double Upstreams Across a Wave

**The Problem:** Double upstreams across a wave have two problems. The first challenge is to make the first upstream feed you onto the wave in the proper place and the second challenge is to make the wave shoot you into the eddy in the proper place for the second upstream. Adjusting your exit from the first wave can easily be done if need be by using a "high-exit" upstream. Convincing the wave to shoot you into the right place though can often be a challenge. The real problem becomes how to surf the wave.

**The Approach:** Approach the first upstream such that on your exit you will be in an ideal position to cross the wave. For the second upstream you want to arrive at the spot with as close to an ideal approach as possible. In effect you want the wave to launch you onto the spot with some speed, an arm's length of room from the inside pole, and you must

## Try This Drill: Speed Surfin'

Surfing is the greatest thing about kayaking and learning to surf waves quickly is one of the most important parts of racing. Find a nice even wave that has eddies on both sides. Try crossing the wave back and forth as quickly as possible. Be sure that each time you cross the wave you open your angle enough that you pierce across the eddyline. Now, each time you are about to fly off the wave and into the eddy, give a solid push on the downstream side so that you jump into the eddy with the boat already spinning upstream. Work on this until you feel the boat carving upstream even before you take your first stroke in the eddy.

Try these different exercises:

* See how few strokes you can take and still rocket into the eddy on each side.
* Try just paddling on a single side each way and then try it with the opposite side. Which side was better heading which way?
* Experiment with how aggressive your angle can be. Are you crossing the wave faster than you had originally thought possible?
* Be a stud and do it all backwards now!

Tip: Crossing a wave quickly can be quite tricky unless you have a clear understanding of where you want to be. The trick to fast wave crossing is to think of the wave as a big ramp. You will be fast if you can always stay on a line that surfs down the ramp, you will be slow if you ever have to climb that ramp:

Think of the level of the eddy as "Waterlevel", this is the mid-point of your wave. If you look carefully at the wave next to your eddy you will see that the distance from the eddyline to the top of the wave is the same as the distance from the eddyline down to the bottom of the trough of that wave. The trick to surfing across that wave quickly is to jump onto the wave as high on the peak of the wave as possible and then run down the wave directly towards the eddyline of the destination eddy. Do not run down into the trough of the wave because you'll then lose some of your momentum as you climb up into the eddy.

To be especially fast, work on carving the boat as you open your angle across the wave. This should cause a "squeeze" effect between your boat and the fast moving current that will rocket you across the wave. Remember to push the bow upstream as you land in the eddy to prevent stalling!

**CROSSING WAVE HERE**
Boat placement on the wave is the most important part of setting up your surf. Photo by Chris Smith.

be spinning upstream!. The most common mistake people make when surfing a wave into an upstream is to peal down across the wave so that they have a downstream rotation to their boat as they cross the wave. If you are not spinning into the gate when you come off the wave you will stall when you reverse your spin.

**The Turn:** The turn at the second upstream is a little tricky because it is likely that you will have a lot of crosscurrent speed coming into the eddy. Be sure to turn your boat sharply out of the gate as soon as you get past the inside pole to prevent sliding into the outside pole.

**The Exit:** A lot happens in a short period of time on these moves. You've just rocketed off a wave, jumped into an eddy and cranked a turn. In spite of all this you must force yourself to launch the boat quickly back into the current. Remember you haven't saved any time until you are quickly headed towards the finish line again!

## Upstreams on a Hole

**The Problem:** There are two kinds of upsteams on holes. We refer to most holes as either "smiling upstream," which is to say the edges of the hole are upstream of middle, or "smiling downstream," which are holes where the edges of the hole are downstream of the middle. These two cases should be treated separately.

## Smiling Upstream

**The approach:** Holes that smile upstream have a curl of water which rolls around the edge of the hole and into the backwash. The curl often looks like a mini-version of the "tubes" surfers in the ocean ride. That curl is the dividing line for your approach. If you are in between the hole and the curl, you will be rocketed into the whitewash behind the hole, do it right and you will land right in the gate. If you are outside of that curl you will be low in the eddy behind the hole-your race is over.

A good approach to an upstream on a hole lands the paddler right in the gate. Photo by Chris Smith.

On your approach you want to attack that curl. The idea is that you will paddle or guide your boat right up the curl and on top of the foam-pile behind the hole. You do this by approaching the curl from above and just a little from the side-your approach line should never be outside of the edge of the curl-and turning into the hole just before you arrive at the trough. This approach has two advantages, you are already spinning and heading in behind the hole before you hit the curl. All you have to do now is simply guide the boat at this point with either a rudder on the inside or a sweep on the outside. Your ideal line is to get as high on the curl as possible so that you land on top of the hole instead of within its grasp.

**The Turn:** As soon as you land in the backwash behind the hole you are going to be violently sucked up into the hole. Do a quick pivoting turn so that you are angled well out of the gate as soon as possible. It is almost always best to hug the inside pole when doing upstreams like this.

**The Exit:** Upstreams on holes are a free-for-all on the exits. Often your best exit stroke is a forward on the inside. Either way do not let yourself be sucked up into the hole until you have reached the edge. If you have to exit across any distance of hole try and paddle across the foam instead of bouncing and losing time in the trough.

## Smiling Downstream

**The Approach:** Holes that smile downstream are like big deflectors that don't want to let anyone in. Make a mistake on one of these upstreams and you are likely to be rejected completely from the backwash. The trick again is to get your boat spinning and coming from the side before you get to the hole, take care of the basics before things get difficult. Every one of these situations is different, but you are looking to do two things on your entry: The first is you want to be on a line which comes down into the hole. Ideally this means you are coming from high enough above the backwash to simply jump over the messy stuff. Otherwise make sure you are not ferrying into these things because you'll need enough angle to pierce the hole without getting stuck in the trough. The second thing you are trying to do is hit the hole with just enough angle to pierce the backwash and enough spin on the boat so that you rotate in behind the gate afterwards. This takes a lot of practice.

**The Turn:** Make this a quick turn and stay tight to the inside pole with angle towards the edge of the hole.

**The Exit:** Run right down the white stuff and peel out. The downward smile of the hole is going to rocket you downstream!

## Advanced

Now that you have mastered boat and stroke placement in many different situations it is time to learn to keep the boat moving. Ideally, as you exit an upstream, you will be going the same speed you were going when you approached the upstream gate. Your coach will refer to this as "carrying your speed through the turn" and it will significantly improve the times of your race runs. There are several ways to tweak your upstream technique so that your boat will better maintain its speed through a turn.

The first of these is to decrease your pivot. A big pivot is a big time loss. The higher the pivot the more time you will waste sitting in the gate. Pivot upstream gates, used in the right place, can be fantastically quick. They can also, if done in the wrong place or the wrong way, leave the paddler looking like he is sitting in molasses.

The second is to completely finish your rotation at the turning point. This is to say, that when you turn your boat, turn it all the way around to where it is facing 45 degrees out of the gate.

Next, work on coming in low enough that you have a full arm's length between your body and the gate. This will give you the room you need to do a powerful draw while you turn the boat. It will also, and this is a big pointer, allow you to sit forward as you pull on your draw stroke, thus accelerating the boat out of the turn. Basically your draw stroke will go in the water out to the side of the boat while you are rotated and sitting up. As you twist the boat around on this stroke feather it forward towards the front of the boat. This is worth trying, you should find that just the fact that you are sitting forward at the end of your draw will keep the boat running out of the eddy.

Lastly, we know from tests that the U.S. participated in at the Colorado Springs Olympic Training center that the first few strokes of a sprint are the most important factor in your sprint time. This is to say that your time from the upstream gate to the next gate will be much quicker if you manage to accelerate quickly out of the upstream as opposed to turning out and then working your way back up to speed. As soon as you start your exit from the upstream then you should follow up your exit with two or three crushingly powerful strokes.

Keep in mind that we are trying to conserve your momentum through an upstream gate. Try a couple of these tests to see if you are doing this well. If you have a coach, have them watch only your head as you do the upstream gate. If your head quits moving, then you have lost your momentum, your boat has stopped moving. If you don't have a coach, then you'll have to decide for yourself how well you are maintaining your speed. A good test that I like is to execute an upstream gate right up to the point where you pull on your first exit sweep. Once you have pulled on your exit sweep quit paddling altogether (keep your shoulders focused on where you're going). If you still exit the gate by tightly wrapping around the inside pole, and you still have forward speed, then you probably have done an excellent upstream.

## Elite

One of my most shocking revelations about upstreams came to me in 1993, the year I won my first World Cup title. I was at the second World Cup race in Lofer, Austria and dead set on nailing down a win to raise my points for the overall title. There was a very tricky upstream gate about midway down the course. It was set in an eddy with a tremendous rip tide so

**BOAT ANGLED OUT OF GATE AT END OF DRAW**
The boat should already be aimed out of the gate at the finish of the draw stroke. Photo by Chris Smith.

that the boaters shot back upstream as they did their turn through the gate. I drove in deep behind the gate, banking into the turn. Then, at just the right moment, I dropped the outside edge snapped a pivot and shot out of the gate. I figured it was one of my best upstreams ever. The T.V. guys were so crazy about it they used the footage as background for all the results for the entire race. I managed to make a copy of the race coverage and bring it home to show the juniors I coach. Just to make a point I took splits of both my upstream gate, and the one Oliver Fix had done. To me the two were opposites. He slunk into the gate with a quite boat, made a subtle low angle pivot and slunk off downstream. He also took 1.2 seconds out of my time! In a single gate!

For you elite folks I have bad news. After years of dreaming about how flashy and dynamic you will be when you finally get to the big time I'm here to tell you that you'll have to temper it down. Sorry about that. Here is the reason why, and listen carefully: turning your boat takes work. Don't believe me? Go out on a lake this very minute and give me twenty minutes of forward sweep/back sweep rotations. How hard you can paddle down a course is almost never the limiting factor to your success in a race. Sure, there are folks who are faster and folks who are slower, but the folks who still have the juice to finish good, quick and precise turns at the end of a racecourse are the ones who will end up on the medal stand again and again. If you really want to get good at this game you need to find a way to make your turning muscles last, which is to say, you need to find out why your turning muscles are getting so tired so quickly.

So here's where I get technical on you. Up untill now when we've talked about conserving our "momentum" through upstream gates, what we really meant was conserving our linear momentum. If you were to paddle across a lake as fast as you can and then quit paddling and simply guide the boat straight ahead it would continue to plow through the water

Technique

**TRY THIS DRILL:**

The two gate upstream drill: Pick two gates to be your two upstream gates. These gates can be on the same wire or one can be more upstream than the other. Now in your mind imagine that there is an invisible line between the inside poles of these two gates. Now, simply start in one of the upstream gates and negotiate the other. Here's the catch. I want you to cross that imaginary line between the gates as quickly as you can on the way to negotiating the second gate. Repeat this drill until you can consistently cross that line directly after you leave the starting gate. This is an excellent drill because if forces a good trajectory between the gates. By crossing the imaginary line as soon as possible you are forcing yourself to have a low exit from the start gate (if you did it right you should be wrapping right around the inside pole of that start gate). You are also, unless you set a demon of a course, setting yourself up for a good wide approach upstream on the next gate. You should, in fact, have the opportunity to paddle on the ideal approach trajectory for that second gate.

**Upstream loops:** Go to a training course on moving water. The feeder canal in D.C. makes a fantastic place to do this workout, although I enjoy doing them anywhere that has easy slow moving current. Set a course with some very easy downstream gates and several, between two and four upstream gates. They can be any kind of upstream you like; ups in the current, ideal eddy, anything. But they must all be the type of gate you can two stroke-only one draw and one sweep after you do your entry sweep. Do loops in sets of ten minutes. That's ten minutes of non-stop medium rate paddling round and round through this same course. The trick is not to go so hard that you are tired, in fact, just the opposite. For the most part go at a pace that you can comfortably paddle the entire time without getting so

tired that your technique begins to fail. This is the equivalent to the sort of pace you would use on an easy jog. Use this pace throughout the gate loop (from the start, through the course, and loop back up to the start again), except in those four upstream gates. In those four upstream gates I want you to paddle like you are five-time World Champion Richard Fox. I want you to cruise in with the ideal approach, I want a crisp draw, and I want a crushingly powerful and precise exit. Then I want you to fall back to your original relaxed pace. Do three to four sets of these 10-minute pieces.

**Whitewater ups:** Here's where it gets a little harder. Go to a good hard whitewater course, someplace that is as hard as the race courses you are training to race on. Now, pick one single upstream gate to work on. This upstream should have something that makes it more difficult than your moving water training gates. It is even better if this upstream gate is set in such big water that you must walk back upstream to re-negotiate it. Now, do this upstream again and again until you get it perfect. Keep this in mind; no matter how impossible a gate seems in a race, someone almost always two strokes it. Try and be this person. Do it with upstreams on big boils, upstreams on eddy lines, upstreams in the current, upstreams on holes, upstreams deep in eddies, etc., etc., etc. You should be a master of two stroking upstreams by the time you start at your next race. I have always said this: if you two stroke all the upstreams you will medal in any race in America. Case in point, my first medal was at the Nationals in South Bend, Indiana. After first runs I was somewhere near twentieth place. For second runs I set the goal that I would two stroke every upstream and finished second behind National Champion Rich Weiss and ahead of the rest of the U.S. team, when I was 16 years old!

even after you were done pushing it. This is your forward linear momentum, it is the same momentum you would have if you were to quit peddling a bicycle and let it roll on down the road. Until now when you did your upstream gates you were hoping to have a little of this momentum left, you were hoping you would finish your turn in an upstream gate and come shooting back into the current on your remaining momentum.

The thing is, there is another type of momentum. Go out again and spin your boat in a circle with some forward and back sweeps. Again, stop paddling and watch as the boat continues to rotate around in a circle. This is your spin momentum. You want to conserve this momentum as well as your forward momentum. Close your eyes now (once you finish reading this) and watch yourself doing your last upstream. You undoubtedly gave yourself a wide approach that landed you right on the "spot." You

then cranked a turn that whipped the boat around so that it was facing out of the gate. You most likely finished this turning draw by converting it to a forward stroke and pulling just a little bit. This most likely made your boat move forward quite nicely towards your exit. It also, most likely, completely killed your turn. Try this the next time you are on the water. Do the upstream gate right up to the point where you finish your draw stroke, and if you normally do this, convert that draw to a little forward stroke. Then stop paddling completely and watch as your boat heads straight up and through the gate. If you want to turn and head towards the finish line you'll need to completely restart this turn again with your exit sweep. Doing this little pull has made you lose your spin momentum.

Now back to bursting your bubble about being flashy. Killing your spin momentum wasn't your only mistake. Throwing in that big ol' flashy turn at the "spot" was the other big mistake. The harder you turn your boat the more you will wear out your turning muscles. Think about being in the weight room. If you were to pick up all the plates you could pick up in one mammoth lift you would only be able to do this once. If you were to cut that by 30% you could probably lift it again and again and again, especially if you only had to lift it a little ways. If you want your turning muscles to last throughout the race run you need to change your paddling style so that you do shorter easier turns. How do you do this? Conserve your spin momentum.

Here's the scoop. Right now you are charging into the "spot" facing parallel to the gate line. You will then put in a draw stroke that turns the boat 135 degrees. You will have pulled on the paddle for this entire stroke and will most likely be spinning so quickly that you need to stop this spin to keep from being shot out of the gate. You will then put in a forward sweep that will restart your turn, again you will be forcing the boat to turn for the entirety of your rotation. To this point you have never let the boat rotate on its own. You have forced that boat to rotate with your own muscles for every little bit of turn. Since you waited till you got to the "spot" to start your boat turning, you were forced to use a mammoth amount of energy to both start the boat turning and to make sure you got out of the gate fast enough. This is the spin momentum equivalent to stopping and starting over and over again.

Now try it like this: As you approach the gate (make sure you are approaching from a wide enough angle to allow room for a sweeping approach), get the boat rotating with a sweep on the outside of your turn. Now, turn and face the spot with a bow rudder on the inside, do not convert this stroke to a forward stroke. This should line you up so that with your next sweep, on the outside, lays you right into the "spot". As you glide into the "spot" let the boat continue to rotate on its own. Let it glide around the turn as you wait for your opening to start you exit. As you see your exit drop in your draw stroke and pull the boat around so that it faces out of the gate. You do NOT need to convert this stroke to a forward stroke. Trust me on this! Quickly switch to your exit sweep and launch yourself out of the gate. If you have done this correctly you have never taken a stroke that does anything to cancel your turn (in practice, you need to use some pull on the inside to line yourself up, but never enough to cancel your turn significantly).

There are several advantages to doing your upstreams this way. The first is that you never have to force a powerful "whipping," all in one spot turn. Instead you do a longer more distributed turn; A turn that never required a maximum effort! Also, because you came into the turn at least parallel to the gate and with a tremendous amount of spin momentum, you did most of your turn in the current as opposed to sitting in the eddy. This is to say that, you used to sit patiently in the pocket of an upstream, every muscle in your body screaming as you man-handled the boat around 135 degrees of

turn, trying to get some sort of an exit trajectory that will give you some relief. Now you come tearing into the upstream, waiting for an exit line while your boat glides towards the "spot" and turns all of its own accord (hopefully with a little help from the eddy!). As soon as you see your exit you crisply crank the boat about 90 degrees, drop an exit sweep and you will not only exit towards the current but will have the spin momentum that allows you to begin paddling without having to force the bow downstream with your muscles. You have just done a shorter, easier, turn. By the time you finish with this book you should be doing shorter easier turns all over the slalom course.

## Offsets

Offsets are the slip'n slide of whitewater slalom. They are the part of our sport where everything happens fast and mistakes quickly compound to disaster. Making short work of these difficult downstream-gate combinations will save you time in the current and give you better approaches to your upstream gates. Learn to do offsets well or you will find they have a way of getting away from you.

The key to offsets is always being prepared for the next gate and success comes from planning ahead so that each gate feeds you into the next. Learn to think of each gate in terms of where you need to be to make the next gate fast and easy. Think of it in terms of an expert billiards player. These players very seldom make incredible shots. Most often good billiards players will make a series of easy shots because each time they sink a ball they leave the que ball in a position that makes the next shot easy. Do the same thing with your offset gates. Your strategy for each offset gate should not only execute that particular gate well, but also leave you in position to make the next gate well. In the bigger picture you will find that every well executed gate, upstream or down, feeds you right into the next gate.

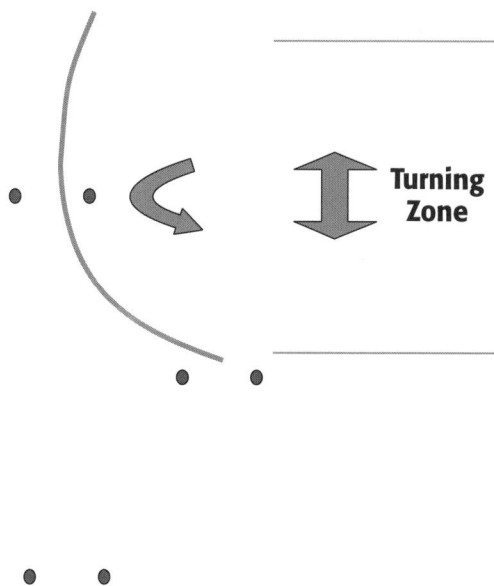

**OFFSET LATE**
A late turn will put you in the second gate with the wrong angle and the wrong trajectory.

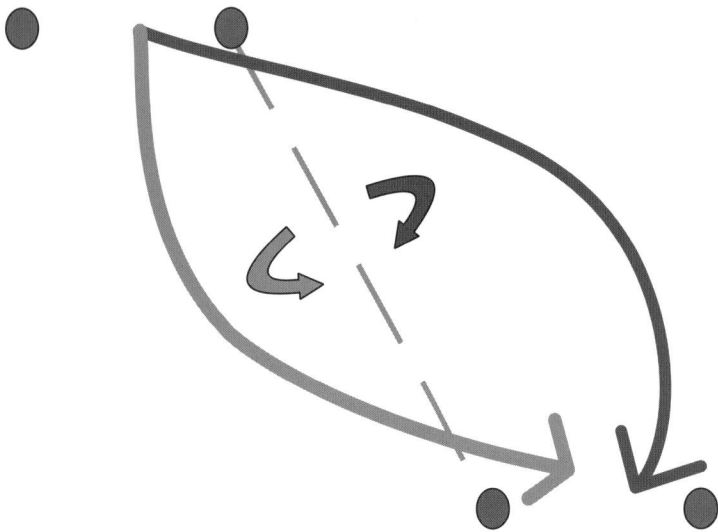

Again with offsets, as with upstreams, the trick is to work from back to front. Start with the last gate and decide where you want to go from there. Do you need to cut back for an upstream on the other side? Do you have open water to run through with no destination for a few seconds? Where you will go next will affect where you need to be in this last gate. Your line after a gate can either be a continuation of the trajectory from the gate before-in which case you can cut your line to the gates so closely that you barely make it-or it can require you to turn a full 180 degrees back in the opposite direction. In this second case you will need a considerable amount of room in order to negotiate the gate in the forward direction. The idea is that you will work backwards through the course setting a plan that negotiates each gate with enough room to then arrive early enough for the next gate. Keep in mind that these things tend to stack up the way you do each gate must give you the room

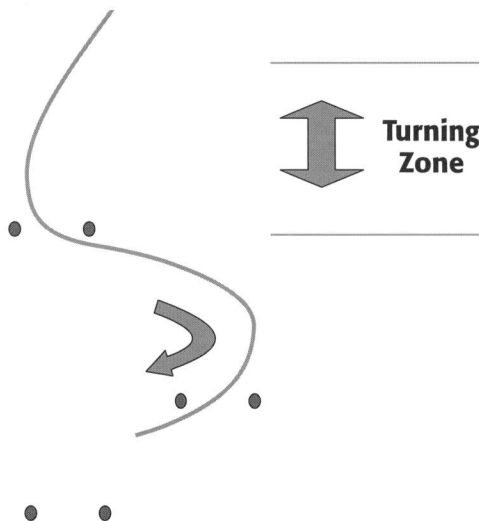

**Turning Zone**

necessary to set up the next turn! In short, at every moment you need to have a plan that makes the next gate easy and also leaves the boat in position to easily negotiate the gate after that. Your whole run should be a linked chain, each move setting you up in the ideal position for the next.

For offsets in particular this means one thing, prepare, prepare, prepare. You must be prepared for each offset. Think of the moving current as a large conveyor belt rushing you towards the finish line. If you waste too much time on a single gate you will ride the conveyor belt past any hope of making the next gate, so don't take that risk. Especially on the first few gates of an offset combination be sure to be over-prepared and well on your way to the next gate by the time you negotiate the first. If you were to draw this out on paper you would see that you are actually negotiating each gate at the end of the turn for that gate! By the time you pass through a particular gate you should already have finished turning towards the next gate and should actually begin turning for the following gate. You are actually making a turn just after gate one that will lead you to gate THREE!

Turns in the current, like the ones you'll use for offset gates are similar to the turns you might make on a ski slope. On a ski slope, for the most part, every time you carve a turn on your skis you will lose altitude down the hill. The same is true of turning in the current. In the time it takes you to cut the boat back from one direction to the other you will be washed downstream. If you start that turn too late or do the wrong type of turn you may get washed past the next gate! Offsets, unlike upstreams, are made even trickier by the fact that most often, if executed well, crossing the gate line should signify the End of your turn.

This means that the hard part of approaching an offset is that you are aiming for a spot above the gate where you will start a turn that finishes at the gate. You are aiming for a point that normally has absolutely no reference point. Where that spot is depends on where you are going and which type of turn you will use. I like to call the area between where I start my turn and where I finish it "the turning zone." Some gates have easy wider approaches and easy exits that make the turning zone quite long. Other gates will be set such that you barely reach them and are then required to immediately turn back. For these types of combinations the turning zone is quite short. In offsets, as with all turns, your boat can really only do some combination of a carving, sliding, or pivot turn. The trick is often deciding which turn to do and when and where to do it.

## The Carving Turn

Carving turns are the hardest but often the fastest way to negotiate offsets. A carving turn involves digging an edge as a sort of skeg so that your boat will grip and carry speed around a turn (see section 3 on how boats turn). The advantage of this is that you can, in hard offset crosses for example, carry your forward momentum through your turn. This can carry you across the current quite quickly without necessitating a lot of re-acceleration.

The disadvantage of this is that these turns must be wider and therefore take more room to set-up. This means the "turning zone", will be quite long, necessitating a lot of space on the approach to carry the boat around the wider turn. These are often not a good way to do tight back-to-back offsets.

## The Sliding Turn

For the most part, you can be turning without actually moving side to side. This can be a real asset in easier gates where you really only want to nip and duck a little to each side. It will also shorten your turning zone. At times its biggest advantage is that you have no grip, so the water has no grip on you and can't push you around when the water is big and unpredictable.

Unfortunately, these are turns that convert little of your speed into the direction you are turning. If you are forced to do one of these turns before a hard cross you'll need to really pull on the paddle to get the boat moving across the current after you negotiate the gate. Paddlers who favor this style tend to do large pushing sweeps followed by quick re-accelerations towards the next gate.

## The Pivot Turn

Pivots are a really good way to turn extremely fast and in one place (remember, this is one place relative to the current. You are still being swept downstream!). These are great turns for quick saves or for harder gate combinations. I usually pivot when I don't have enough room to carve, but still need some speed. This works especially well if you can turn far enough above the gate to start the boat heading back towards the next gate using the sterns "squirt" effect to accelerate the boat as you come out of the turn. Pivot turns have an extremely short turning zone.

The problem with pivot turns is that they carry much less speed through a turn and they require you to put a whole lot of spin into your boat. Often it is hard to stop this spin and you waste both time and energy just to cancel out all the energy you put into that spin. It is not uncommon to use a strong pivot turn on one of the earlier gates in an offset and then find yourself desperately fighting that same turn when you want the boat to stop spinning. Learn to be good at all three of these turns and I guarantee you will have an advantage over your pivot happy competitors.

## Basic Offsets

**The Approach:** By the time you are approaching this first offset gate you should have a plan for the entire combination of gates in front of you. Too often you will have open water or an easy approach to this first gate and will use that opportunity to rev up your engines and head directly for the gate. Do not charge right at this gate. You must head for the

**SHIPLEY OFFSET**
Early on offsets are characterized by wide approaches to adequately prepare for the next gate. Photo by Chris Smith.

**Turning Zone**

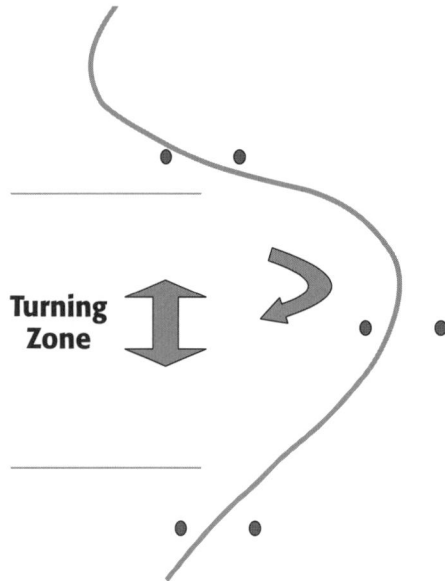

**The Exit:** The single thing that matters on this exit is that you begin to turn your boat downstream towards the next gate. Even at the highest levels of slalom people make this mistake time and time again. Here is the crazy thing about it. Read this carefully because it sounds far fetched. If you are turning downstream between two offsets you will actually cross the river higher than if you are turning upstream! You make the offsets easier by turning down the entire way from one gate to another! If you arrive at the gate you are negotiating with the necessary angle to turn downstream towards the next gate you will be further upstream and you will have a better approach angle to the next gate. As a general rule in offsets you will find that you want to turn down towards the next gate as you are negotiating the first one.

## Tight Three-Gate Offsets

**The Problem:** It is not uncommon to have three offsets set so tightly that it is almost impossible to make the three separate turns before you are washed downstream past one or more of the gates. You can do these three gates with only a single turn!

**The Solution:** You are going to really want to set this first gate up. Make your approach well wide of this first gate so that as you are coming up to the gateline you are already heading above the second gate of the offset. As you cross the gateline of this first gate begin your turn back for the THIRD GATE! You leave gate one turning hard towards gate three, simply make your turn wide enough to duck into gate three. I can often do all three gates on the single draw I take after the first gate.

## Dive Gates

**The Problem:** Dive gates, or downstreams in eddys are tricky. You are often dealing with strong currents and strong eddylines and things happen very quickly. Make a mistake on one of these gates and you'll drive yourself crazy trying to untangle yourself both from the gate and the eddy.

Set up a dive gate so that you are already turning out of the eddy when you cross the eddyline. Avoid changing the direction of your turn in the slow eddy-water.

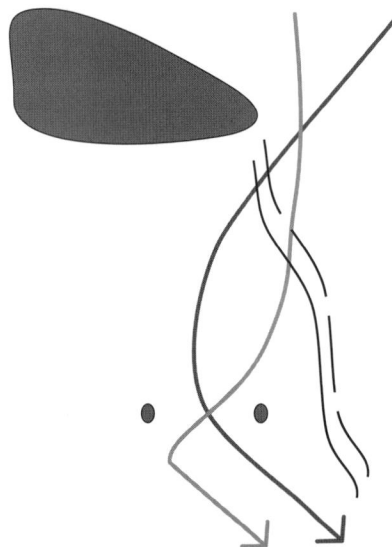

**The Solution:** Dive gates have their own set of rules and if you can follow them you are usually the quickest on that split:

Try and make it a straight line through the gate and back into the current. This can often be done by jumping right next to the rock and landing with the right angle and trajectory to run right back to the current.

Never reverse a turn in an eddy. If you come into an eddy and let it turn your boat towards shore you are going to have to kill the boat's speed if you want to get it headed back out of the eddy again. Do what you need to do so that when you enter the eddy you are already arcing back towards the current! If you are still turning in towards the eddy as you cross the eddyline you will stall when you try and get back to the current.

point on the river where you will begin your turn for the next gate. Your approach should allow a "turning zone" where you can complete your turn before you cross the gate line. Keep in mind your linked turns. You are heading for a spot far enough above the gate that you will have time to complete your turn by the time you arrive between the poles. Make sure you give yourself enough room, if you have it, to carry speed through this turn. You will need that momentum as you head across to the next gate.

**The Turn:** The turn is usually the hard part of this move. Think a lot about the "turning zone." Giving yourself a turning zone means that you will aim to arrive far enough upstream of the gate that you can finish your turn before you drift between the poles! This is best learned on easy slower water so that you can learn to adequately judge how much room you'll need to arc your boat around and aim it ABOVE the next gate before you go between the poles of this first gate.

## An Eddy Between Two Downstreams

**The Problem:** An eddy between two offsets can cost a racer a lot of time. The trick is to set up a trajectory that will slingshot you into the eddy on the approach and will re-accelerate you when you leave the eddy on the far side.

If you approach this downstream combination from above, use the eddy to turn you and catapult you into the current on the other side. If you are coming from the side you should attack the eddy and push your bow downstream to avoid being spun out by the eddyline.

**The Solution:** There are two situations for your approach to this eddy. Draw a forty-five degree angle upstream from the point you will enter the eddy. You will have a different approach depending on whether you approach the eddy above or below this line. If you are approaching from above this forty-five degree angle you will want to slingshot off the eddy by letting it turn you across the eddy as you pierce the eddyline. Do not jump if you are on this approach! It will just make you stall.

If you are approaching from below this forty-five degree angle you will want to turn the other way-down into the eddy-so that you carry speed across the eddy. In fact, the danger here is that you will be turned upstream by the eddy! You want to pierce that eddyline so cleanly that you no longer have to use turning strokes as you cross the eddy.

The eddy you crossed should slow your boat down considerably. To help the boat re-accelerate leave yourself a little room on the second gate. This way you can use the current to re-accelerate the boat by turning downstream as you leave the eddy.

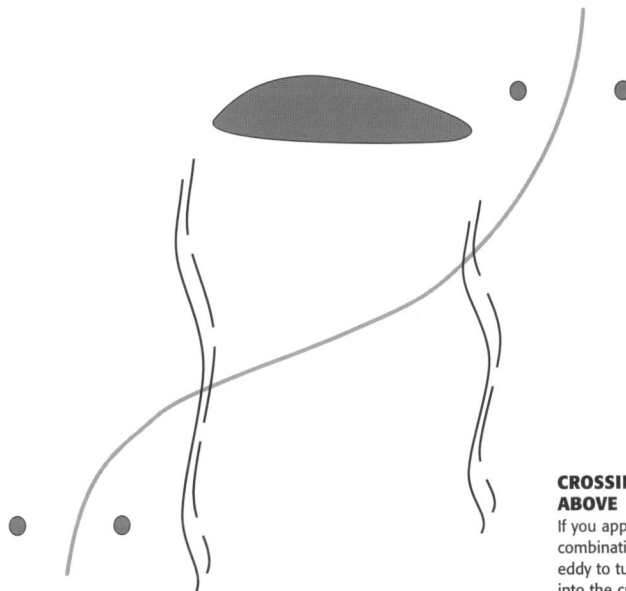

## Reverse Gates

**The Problem:** There are many reasons to do reverse gates but the most common is because the course is too tight to negotiate the gates directly. This means that you are either doing the reverse gate because you barely made it to this gate or else you are doing a reverse gate to give yourself more room with which to execute the next move.

**The Solution:** There are two separate solutions for these two separate situations. In the first case, if you arrive late to this gate and simply want to get turned and head downstream you should push the boat downstream as you turn. This is done by leaving the boat flat and actually facing your blade such that you push yourself towards the finish line as you turn. Ideally you would like to finish your turn as soon below the gate as you can.

In the second and more common situation, you are trying to better prepare yourself for the next move. This is a complicated maneuver so again we will break it down and look at the approach, the turn, and the exit.

**The Approach:** The reason you are doing a reverse gate in this situation is that you cannot afford to drift downstream as you turn. As such your approach should be as much as possible from the side. This will stall your downstream momentum just as you arrive at the gate.

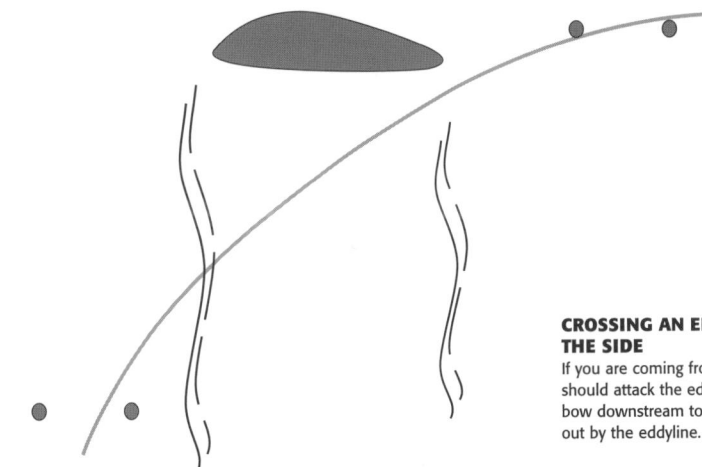

**CROSSING AN EDDY FROM ABOVE**
If you approach this downstream combination from above, use the eddy to turn you and catapult you into the current on the other side.

**LEE DOING BAD EDDY CROSS**
Pierce the eddyline to avoid being spun out. Photo by Chris Smith.

**CROSSING AN EDDY FROM THE SIDE**
If you are coming from the side you should attack the eddy and push your bow downstream to avoid being spun out by the eddyline.

**The Turn:** The turn is a bit complicated. Because of the way you are approaching the gate the most effective lead-in stroke is a stern draw. This should slide your stern out and leave your boat facing just short of straight upstream in the gate. As soon as you are above the center of the gate turn your entire torso such that you are watching the inside pole! This will leave the gate in your blind spot for a period of time but will make your turn much quicker. Reach through the gate with your draw and , this is the most important part, turn the boat past straight upstream! The most common time loser in reverse gates is leaving the boat facing straight upstream. If the boat faces upstream you will sit dead in the water for at least a second. If you turn the boat so that it begins to ferry out of the gate on its own you will gain precious time while you switch from your draw stroke to your exit sweep.

**The Exit:** Your exit should be a powerful sweep that pushes you directly where you would like to head. If done properly this stroke should simply accelerate the boat in the direction it is already heading. C-1's are typically the best example to watch for proper gate technique. These boats are scrambling to make up time in these gates because half of their competitors can often simply do the move direct.

## Advanced

We have already talked about turning before each gate of an offset and then trying to turn down towards the following gate. As you get better it is time to force yourself to execute offset gates in this manner. Top athletes do this by aiming their boat above the next offset gate and forcing the bow downstream as they pass between the poles. The bow is forced down by taking a strong sweep stroke on the inside of your turn—this is the upstream side of the boat as you finish your turn for the current gate.

I have worked a little bit with Australian coach Mike Druice. We once discussed the importance of learning this basic method of offsets. He told me that, after years of working with athletes at all levels, he had found that no one ever became proficient at offsets until they had mastered this method. The hard thing to explain to them, he said, was that the best folks rarely did their offsets this way.

## Elite

I divide the way I do offsets into three different types and name them after the people who do them best. The first way is my way, the way I did offsets in the early '90's by carving the boat in wide arcs and always giving myself the preparation I needed to make the next gate easy. I would sit upright and sink an edge so that the boat continually tracked in a best-fit curve through all the gates.

The second way is the "Fox" way and is a tighter line where the paddler aims more directly at the next gate. The paddler turns sharply with draws and short quick pivots before accelerating out of the turn with quick sharp strokes. Again the paddler is upright in the boat.

The final type of offsets I call "Ratty" offsets and are the desperate nipping and tucking offsets that

## TRY THIS DRILL: Ski Slalom Offsets

Choose an area of your course that would be a good place to work on offsets. Before you begin your workout pull all the gates over and tie one of the poles up out of the way on the crossbar. This will leave you with five or six single pole offsets in your course. Your slalom course should look a little like a ski slalom course.

Now, line those poles up in a straight line in the current-I do mean a straight line here. Your challenge is to negotiate this entire five or six gate course by only putting your paddle in the water a single time for each pole that you pass. For each pole you are allowed to do a single draw stroke which will turn your boat so that it is aimed above the next pole and then you are allowed to convert that draw into a sweep as you go underneath that single pole which will push you across the current and turn your boat downstream. Then you are allowed to rotate your body and do a single draw which will rotate your boat so that it is aimed above the third pole. Repeat this combination for each pole. You should be very strict about putting your paddle in the water a single time per pole! Even if your wires are spaced so far apart that you must drift for a while you should wait it out and negotiate this entire five or six pole course while only dipping your paddle in the water a single time per pole!

Stroke combinations, degree of preparation, and a myriad of other factors will evolve in time. The basic boat trajectory and spin however will not. The wild dodging offsets you will see on the World Cup circuit will actually have more in common with this basic offset than you would ever believe possible.

The next step is to learn how and where to cut some of those corners when you can. It is time now to learn to cut the fat out of your offsets so that you are merely doing the bare essentials necessary to making these specific gates. One thing I can't emphasize enough though, you must be able to do those basic offsets perfectly if you are going to be able to make these shortcuts work.

On today's racing scene Paul Rattcliffe and I quite often trade places for first place from race to race. Though we often have similar times, most people would say that we have radically different styles in offsets. Typically I would favor a more basic offset where I am over-prepared, sitting upright, and linking turns through the offsets (check out how good I make myself look!).

Paul on the other hand will most often slither through an offset narrowly placing his head between the poles as he charges directly from one to the other head ducking each gate and cutting every corner to its utmost limit. Even I will admit that we look nothing alike.

Here is the crazy thing, he and I have more in common in the way we do our offsets than either of us do with almost anybody else out there. Our strokes, our body position, even our boat position are quite often different throughout most of the offset, but at the few key places where the paddler's stroke, trajectory, and position matter, we are dead even.

You may find that neither one of us are doing the specific stroke combination described above, but at that key place just downstream of the inside pole we are both in the same place and desperately pushing our bow downstream in one way or another. These are the places you need to find and prepare for. You will find that in any gate combination there are a couple of key places where you need to be in the right place and doing the right thing. What happens between these places should be made easy by your execution of the previous move and should be done with the objective of setting you up for the next move.

Paul Rattcliffe has mastered. Paul aims the boat very directly through and offset and slides the boat with quick stern draws to maneuver between the poles. This is most often the quickest way through short and tight offsets. Here is a more focused look at each of these methods:

For every offset you need two things, angle and momentum. The angle will allow you to take off in the direction you need to go. If you arrive in the gateline of any gate in an offset without the angle necessary to already be heading to the next move, you are in trouble. The second thing you need is momentum. The harder the offsets are, the more momentum you need headed towards the next move. This is to say the harder the offsets are going to be the more you are going to want to arrive at the gateline of one offset already headed quickly towards the next offset. The opposite is also true for both of these factors: the easier the offset is the less time you want to spend preparing your angle and momentum when you could just be heading towards the finish line.

So every offset, depending on its degree of difficulty, will require a different amount of preparation and a different strategy for success. The easiest offsets can be sprinted through while the hardest offsets are often so hard that you will go far out of your way to carefully prepare your approach.

I use three different strategies for offsets, depending on their degree of difficulty. These strategies are modeled off of three different styles of paddler I mentioned. For the really hard offsets I use the style I grew up doing: wide swooping approaches with lots of carve to conserve my momentum and lots of angle so I have extra room to keep the boat running. These are the so-called "Shipley offsets." For my in between offsets, offsets that are difficult but ones which will still allow me to keep my paddling I use what I think of as "Fox" offsets. This style of paddling was something we were all taught to mimic when I was growing up. These allow the paddler to remain sitting up and to continue his normal rhythm of strokes, but are shorter crisper turns with more sliding than carving. Finally the short quick offsets, especially when the gates are quite close together and require quick reac-

A Shipley offset is characterized by extra preparation and wide carving turns. This style is best for difficult offsets where you need cross-current speed to make it to the next gate. Photo by Chris Smith.

## FOX OFFSETS
Fox's offsets are characterized by crisp clean lines with no extra preparation but also without the risky tight lines seen in Rattcliffe's style. Photo by Chris Smith.

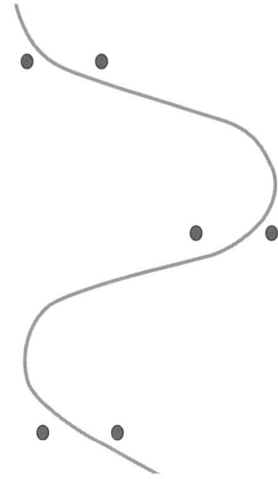

tions and nimble strokes. For these offsets I use a style that mimics Paul Rattcliffe with his powerful sweeps combined with quick ducks of the head from side to side to keep himself in the gates.

## The Shipley Offset

Essentially this was the original offset that I went through above (see photos). Give yourself a large "turning zone" above the gate so that you can use a carving turn on your approach. The key to these offsets is that you arrive in the gate already carrying speed towards the next gate and that you already have the angle necessary to head directly to the next gate! The essence of maneuver is that the entire preparation for the gate was done above the gate.

## The Fox Offset

Fox offsets are more direct, but the paddler still finishes their turn above the gate and they still pass through the middle of the gate.

Richard Fox was a crisp and precise paddler. His offsets were theepitome of his style. A typical Richard Fox offset would have a much more direct approach than Shipley offsets. He would tend to run his boat directly to the start of the turning zone and then begin a crisp pivoting/sliding turn that would carry itself through the gate. The important thing about this type of offset was that Richard still went far enough wide of the inside pole that he was able to, without bobbing his head, carry speed back through the gate towards the next gate. The way he affected the turn though was by beginning the turn with a crisp sharp draw that turned his boat, as the pivot released, shot him towards the next gate. However he would finish the turn after the gate with a sweep on the outside. Thus in a "Fox" offset you would have momentum towards the next gate but would still need to finish the turn as you were crossing the gateline.

## Rattcliffe Offset

Paul Rattcliffe may very well be the quickest paddler ever to climb into a kayak. His ability to nip and tuck and dive from gate to gate is unparalleled in canoe slalom. Since I, like most people, lack the ability to take the risks Paul takes on a full-time basis I

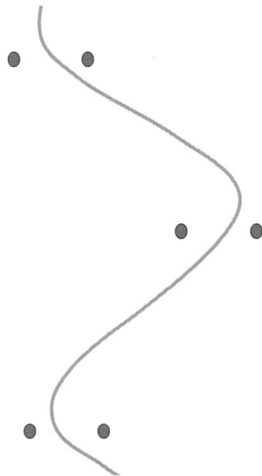

Fox's offsets are characterized by crisp clean lines with no extra preparation but also without the risky tight lines seen in Rattcliffe's style.

**RATTY OFFSET**
Rattcliffe offsets are tight, risky and exceptionally fast in some cases. Photo by Chris Smith.

prefer to only borrow his radical style when necessary. Let me tell you though, when the offsets are bunched together with only the room to make a half-stroke correction per gate it is easy to become a believer in this radical style.

Essentially Paul's offsets are quite similar to Richard's except they are done a full stroke earlier. Where Richard would do a strong draw just above the gate and then reach through the poles to finish the turn with a quick sweep, Paul will do a quick draw above the gate and then a powerful sliding sweep through the gate as he sits back to put his head between the poles. The advantage to Paul's style is that, by sliding his stern out with his powerful draw he can "shimmy" his boat from side to side quite quickly without having to paddle it back and forth so much. Essentially his turns give the boat all the necessary angle but the paddler will have almost no momentum towards the next gate. This is a great solution for quick offsets when you do not have to traverse very far across the current between gates.

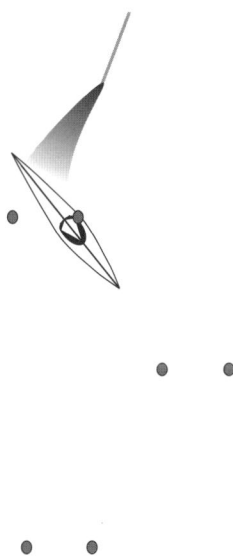

**RATTCLIFFE OFFSETS**
Aim right for the inside pole on a Rattcliffe offset. Sliding your stern out at the last second will move you into the gate.

# The Training

*"Whitewater slalom? I guess you must train a little to get here."*
    *-Unknown Olympic Swimmer to Scott Shipley at the 2000 Olympic games.*

**TRY THIS DRILL**

**How wide can you go?**

Set a course of easy offsets on a relatively featureless part of the river. You are looking for the part of your course where the water is moving, possibly with smaller waves, but is devoid of mid-current eddies and holes. Your offset course should be easy enough that you can execute a perfect run at your current ability level.

Do runs on the course until you are completely satisfied with your ability to execute flawless runs. Your runs should not be in the least bit desperate or rushed. You are trying, on this first course, to get to the point where you are effortlessly carving your way through the course.

Now, change the course by moving each of the offsets out by half of a gate-width. You should be making the course minimally harder without changing it so much that you must alter your technique to compensate for the added difficulty. Run this course repeatedly until you have now mastered this harder course with equally relaxed and controlled technique.

Incrementally increase the difficulty of this same course throughout the workout. You should find that you are able to maintain perfect technique and ample control on courses that are much harder than you had originally thought possible. In the end you will eventually find that the course is a desperate scramble to keep yourself in the gates and headed towards the finish. Again, work to maintain your technique while also adapting to the difficulty of the course. This is my favorite part of the workout.

## Yearly Training Plan

If you are a serious full time training athlete your year will be filled with hour after hour of grueling, cold, intense workouts. Day after day, regardless of weather or water conditions, regardless of holidays and weekends, you will get up in the morning put on your wet smelly paddling gear and walk down to the river for another workout. In the end I found that it was the rigors of daily training that I loved most about slalom, but having said that I must confess that the joy of training, by itself, would not have kept me in this sport for so long. The truth is, if you train, you want results. Unfortunately, just being dedicated enough to go out, day after day, isn't going to win the Olympics. You will not see results based on effort posted at your next team trials. It is not enough to simply train harder than you competition to beat them-you must train better.

Take a look around at the athletes you train with. Think about the extremes of your training group. Every training squad seems to have that athlete that trains and trains, working far beyond the point where they can maintain adequate technique. This athlete most often is built like a rock but never seems able to keep their boat on line. If you were to watch every workout they did you would find, just like it would do to the rest of us, their training has worn them out. They are so tired and working so hard that it is impossible for them to maintain good technique. For hour after hour, week after week, these athletes are training and practicing bad technique. These people tend to love the work more than the paddling and their technique is often clunky and over-muscled. They are often slower because they have practiced muscling their way through a slalom course instead of finessing their way down it.

Every training group also has those folks who are just the opposite. These people favor technique and short races to the longer, more grueling workouts. These paddlers are often quite nimble and quick but lack the ability to maintain their speed over a full-length course. Their technique is most often risky and prone to massive blowouts. Oddly enough, these paddlers are also quite often tired and unable to paddle at top speed. This is not only because they are less fit than the other paddlers, but because they are repeatedly training the same physical system again and again. Simply put, there is only so much high intensity work a body can do before it is torn up and must either rest, or else go slower. These paddlers could be letting their lactic and strength systems rest at the same time they were working-at a considerably lower pace-their aerobic systems.

In everything in life, there is a shorter, easier path to get where you want to go, and a longer, harder path that is less efficient, less effective, and less fun. Training is exactly the same; there is an easy way to get better and many harder ways to get better. The harder the path you choose to the top, the less likely it will work. Reaching the top in our sport means continually focusing your training. To be the best you must continually take the time to chart a path from where you are to where you want to be. This is not to say that the best paddlers are the ones who train the least, they are the ones who train the best. A common algorithm for high school coaches is to simply figure out how much your competition is training and then simply do more. As if training more automatically means you will perform better. This is true to a point, but in the bigger picture it is the athlete who trains better that will win.

But what does training better mean? Better training can mean a lot of things. Better training means making your technique workouts as focused as possible. Better training means incorporating those technique lessons into the rest of your workouts. Better training means learning what sort of fitness your body needs to perform on race day, and then learning how to shape your training to best meet those physical needs. Part of your quest for success in slalom should include constantly striving to find new and better ways to train

Beware of where find this info. You will find that there is a tremendous amount of resources out there to teach you about how to make your body fit that are difficult to relate to slalom. There is a lot of literature out there concerning training your body's strength, lactic, and aerobic systems. Despite their complexity, paddlers often seek to implement these ideas into their training. The challenge lies in incorporating good training ideas into a good slalom training plan. These books can tell you how to get better at lifting weights, or paddling across a lake, or how to make your body a more efficient lactic or aerobic engine. The thing almost none of these books can tell you though is how to train to become the best slalom athlete in the world. These authors know nothing concerning the advantages of training on whitewater versus flatwater, they ignore the benefits of nailing two stroke upstreams time and time again. It is up to you to mesh the physical needs of slalom with the technical ones. It is up to you to put together your own training plan.

This is not to say that you shouldn't research some aspects of your training plan. In fact I encourage you to do so. Most top athletes in our sport have spent a

Photo by Chris Smith.

lifetime doing just that. What follows is a very general summary of the way these top whitewater athletes train. This is a rough guide, both physically and technically, to whitewater slalom training today.

## Learning Technique

Rodeo in 1993 changed radically from what it had ever been before. The boats became half the size they had been before, people began to train, and companies pumped unheard of dollars into the sport in preparation for its World Championship debut in America. As you would expect, all of these factors contributed to radically improve the difficulty of acrobatics and the degree of excellence with which these moves were executed.

Eric Jackson and myself, both teammates in slalom events, had spent the summer in Europe racing while the rodeo crowd prepared and trained at Hell Hole for the upcoming World Championships. By the time

Photo by Chris Smith.

our sport. Discovering the easiest most efficient way will save you time and effort in the long run. Learn to maximize your training time by making these few things a habit in every workout:

## EVERY WORKOUT NEEDS A GOAL

The one single thing you can do to increase the amount of technique you learn is to spend the time off the water deciding what it is you wish to learn. Identify what your weaknesses are and make it the goal of your training to improve these skills. Think about this in relation to every other skill you learn. Have you ever had a schoolteacher tell you to spend the year putting whatever you want down on paper? No! Every lesson had a purpose and the sum of these lessons taught you what you needed to know. You can learn paddling the same way yet every day I see paddlers training on randomly designed courses. Time and again I see paddlers do an entire hour's work with no objective to their work. This is a waste of time! When I start a workout I have a set objective that I want to work on, for example I want to keep the boat moving in tight approach upstreams. Now, every course I design is filled with different cases of tight approach upstreams. By taking the time to give this workout an objective I have done several things. I have taken the time to identify a skill that I am executing poorly. I have focused both my course design and analysis on that one thing, and I have taken responsibility for learning that skill. I guarantee you that I will be doing better tight approach upstreams by the end of that workout. This has to be a better method than setting interesting courses and hoping that they will coincidentally help you race better that summer.

In contrast, also make time to train to your strengths. If you are particularly good at a certain skill-whether it be pivots or strength, or what have you-then find ways to work that into your technique. The idea is to improve your weaknesses while thriving on your strengths!

## CONSTANTLY EVALUATE YOURSELF

Keep this one thing constantly in mind as you are training. No matter how hard you are working, no matter how many workouts you are getting in, somebody is training harder. You must constantly be analyzing both how you are training and how you are paddling. Be critical and be hard on yourself. You must learn to demand excellence of yourself.

Here is a fantastic example of what I mean. When I was growing up out in the Northwest I lived on a peninsula, a peninsula that had no rivers within an hour and a half of where I lived. I was forced to train, up till the point that I turned eighteen and went off to college, on a daily basis on saltwater with only a single gate!

Every weekend however, I would drive off to one of the best whitewater training sites in the world. I was able to spend two days a week training with some of the top paddlers on one of the top courses anywhere. Since I was so competitive, I was constantly trying to find ways to make my flatwater training during the

both of us arrived, about two weeks before the event, people were doing things that were unheard of just four months before when we had qualified for the team. It became obvious in the first couple of training sessions that we were completely outgunned by our competitors in every way.

Yet by the time of the competition a couple of weeks later, Eric was a virtually unbeatable and I finished second behind him. We had learned rodeo better in two weeks than any of the others had in the entire summer! What was it about Eric and I that allowed us to catch up a summer's worth of work in such a short time? Technique training!

Both of us, in our slalom lives, had spent a lifetime learning to learn technique. We had an advantage over the rodeo crowd because we knew what to look for and how to use training tools like coaching and video to pick out the things that actually mattered and learn them!

There is an easy way and a hard way to learn to do

week more effective so that I would be faster the following weekend when I went up against the boys. I would force myself every Monday morning to think about the one thing that I needed to work on most. I had to find the one thing that I was the worst at that previous weekend and then find a way to improve that skill.

Let me tell you this now, most people like to work on what they are good at, not what they necessarily need to practice the most. The best champions are constantly trying to rid themselves of their faults, not just practice their strengths.

## TAKE RESPONSIBILITY FOR YOUR OWN TECHNIQUE

My coaches will tell you that I am one of the most frustrating athletes to work with in the whole world. I am constantly scheduling my own workouts, changing the focus of workouts that have been set long before, and deciding for myself what, where, and how I will train. Here is the reason why: YOU ARE RESPONSIBLE FOR MAKING SURE YOU ARE FAST. Your coaches may or may not coach you on a daily basis and they may or may not have a plan put together that will make you a World Champion as soon as possible. You must take this responsibility!

I have seen too many athletes who show up on a daily basis and ask the coach what they should do for training, what their focus should be, what they are good or bad at. Coaches and training partners are tremendous training tools but you must maintain control of your own training. Only you will know if you have mastered a certain skill, only you will know if you are truly comfortable with a certain type of move, and believe me, when the starter waves you into the starting gate only you will be there to paddle the boat.

Taking responsibility for your own training is setting goals for your workouts, it is evaluating your training and your paddling, but it is also taking responsibility for making sure these things are done right. Somebody must take responsibility for making sure that you are prepared for your race-that person has to be you. It is my belief that only by taking full responsibility for your training, and by being supremely self-confident, that you can truly leave the starting gate focused on winning.

*"You must assume responsibility for choosing to pursue power. Know that you alone have chosen to be tested, and then proceed without doubt, remorse, or blame. You alone are responsible"*
-Mike Livingston to Olympic Gold Medallist Brad Lewis. (Assault on lake Cassitas, pg. 95)

## MASTER THE BASICS

There are many tricks to our sport and you will need to spend a lifetime discovering what they all are. In the end you will most likely decide that the basis for every well-executed move were well-executed strokes, leans, and body position. The truth is that almost all of us learned the basics from some kid who got paid five dollars an hour to teach beginners to be competent. We have all improved well past that

point but at some point you must go back and re-learn the things that you now take for granted.

You will most likely do well over 200 strokes per race run. You must be executing those strokes at their peak of efficiency and power before you can effectively master good technique. I spend about six workouts a month working on either basic strokes, or basic technique with a single gate! Take the time to constantly maintain your basics regardless of how talented you have become.

## TAILOR YOUR ENTIRE SCHEDULE TO THE MASTERING OF TECHNIQUE

Technique workouts are not the sole realm of technique training. I keep my technical focus throughout my training. If I am still working on tight-approach upstreams for example, I will set full-length courses that have a tight-approach upstream. I will put tight-approach upstreams in my loops workouts and when I warm-up I will concentrate on my flexibility and rotation so that I can over-rotate on the approach to these upstreams. I think you see my meaning here. Tight-approach upstreams will permeate every facet of my training until I have perfected that maneuver and moved on to something new.

There is actually a lot of evidence to support that this is actually the most efficient way to work on technique. Oliver Fix and his coach Helmet Hanschuh would always include technical moves in their long endurance sessions since they had read that this is the best and longest lasting way to learn technique. Here is an example of this sort of training:

In 1999 I began working with a German paddler named Hella Pannewig. She was the fourth boat on the German team but had finished in the top four in World Cup races the previous year. She also had had several discouraging runs that same season. After the season was over we decided that her paddling lacked any spring to it. Basically her runs were done entirely at one pace the whole way down the course. If she stayed on line she would have fantastic times, but if she got behind somewhere on the course and needed to speed up or pause to get back on line, then she was in trouble. Hella lacked the ability to change pace and the power to spring forward to where she needed to be.

In looking at her training plan over the previous years we saw that she spent almost her entire fall and winter working primarily at long, slow, endurance in monstrous volumes. She would do up to seven or eight steady-state workouts a week that were longer than 60 minutes! Her plan maintained this volume, although with shorter and shorter workouts up till the day of the race. We decided that there were several things she needed to do to improve her ability to change pace. First she needed to train less so that she would have the energy to pick up the pace when she needed to. She also needed to train her muscles to sprint by gaining both strength and power (weights and sprints). Lastly, she needed to train the technique of when and how to sprint so that she would have the experience to accelerate when she needed to.

To achieve these goals we changed her training in several ways. We took a few of her long endurance workouts out of her typical workweek. The others we shortened so that she would not be doing so much work in a week. We also changed these workouts from being straight ahead flatwater workouts to being hybrid workouts. These were workouts where she would pass through a slalom course about once every three minutes or so.

As you would expect we also set the courses so that she had a couple of moves where she needed to sprint to keep the boat moving (either downs in eddys or a particularly hard offset). In addition we also added two workouts a week where she was doing sprints against a funnel. This helped to build the strength and the power she would need to effectively move the boat when she needed to.

In the gym we changed her weight routine from what was largely muscular endurance to being a program that was entirely a maximum strength workout. We never let this issue disappear from our focus whether we were training lactic, technique, or endurance. Despite its presence in some of our focused workouts this is an example of a technical goal that we worked almost entirely independently from our technique workouts.

### PRIORITIZE TECHNICAL TRAINING ABOVE EVERYTHING ELSE

I always thought that one of the funniest things about training with people was how seriously they take their weight training routines. Virtually every paddler who seriously weight trains will constantly put aside everything else to make sure they make those weight workouts. There are tons of studies that prove, within a minute degree of accuracy, that if you miss a weight workout you will be some amount weaker by the time you get to your big race. Many of these same paddlers will actually decrease the amount of technical workouts they do in favor of doing more weight workouts, again to match all the

Photo by Chris Smith.

scientific data in hundreds of periodicals.

I've got news for you, nobody studies kayaking, nobody knows how much you'll lose if you let your technical workouts slip a little. Nobody can say for sure how much of an effect this will have on your season. I will say this though, and this I know for sure, Technique must be your number one priority all year long. You must constantly strive for perfection. You must never let anything take priority over your mission to master the sport of whitewater kayaking. Time and time again I see races lost simply because a paddler lacked the proper angle in a single gate! Focus first on having the most precise technique you can possibly imagine. Then lift weights in your spare time.

## STRENGTH TRAINING

### PHYSICAL OBJECTIVES OF STRENGTH TRAINING

Almost everyone assumes that weight training is a must, and a mainstay, for any serious training program. I have found that this is not necessarily true. A good training program, at its very heart, is based on specific goals or objectives. Most training plans then have a multi-faceted approach to meeting those goals. Each part of a training regime targets at least one, if not more, of the athlete's objectives. Weight training, in the context of an elite slalomist's training plan, should only be thought of as one small part in a larger whole. Its importance, or lack thereof, should be weighed against the priorities of the whole

In my training plan, weight training serves a very specific list of objectives. I use weights to gain strength and to avoid injuries. This means that my program is focused on building muscles that are directly or indirectly affected by paddling. Those muscles directly affected by paddling are worked to gain maximum strength in the movements I do IN THE BOAT.

In-the-boat strength is increased three ways. First, the obvious way, by breaking the muscle down to increase the cross section of muscle fiber, i.e. make the muscle stronger. Every time you train hard you'll tear the muscles a little and they will heal to become a stronger muscle. Second by training the muscles to perform the specific paddling movements-thereby teaching the separate muscle groups to coordinate, or work together. This is the "summation of forces" that Bill Endicott was talking about. You will be surprised how much more powerful you can become by simply incorporating your larger muscle groups into strokes normally done by your arms. Lastly, this strength training will train more muscle fibers to "fire" per effort (the muscles only allow you to "recruit" so many fibers, training the muscle to recruit a larger percentage of fibers increases strength).

Those muscles not directly used by paddling, the non-specific muscles, are worked to provide an overall balance in the body. Strength imbalances created by only training paddling muscles can often lead to chronic sports injuries. If you want a great example of this, try training twice a day for a year, and then throw a baseball as hard as you can. Most of you, if you don't do serious damage, will notice a lot of pain associated with this simple exercise. The reason for this is that you are using, in part, muscles that have grown quite strong from paddling. The rest of the muscles you use to throw will be ones that are largely neglected in the boat. The combination of extremely powerful muscles pulling on weaker ones will be quite painful. Your training plan should create some balance of fitness throughout your body.

There are really two different strength systems that you can work in your training. The most obvious is your peak strength. This is your body's ability to exert its extreme amount of force-but only for a single repetition. When you see the strong man at the circus pick up a couple of mules one or two times he is using his peak strength.

The second system you can work is your muscular endurance-your body's ability to move at some percentage of its peak strength-for a long period of time. In the weight room your peak strength can be improved by lifting at 75% or greater of your one lift maximum for that exercise. Most likely you would only be able to do ten or less repetitions at this sort of resistance. Your muscular endurance work would be done typically at 65% or lower. Often muscular endurance lifts are done in circuit training or as timed sets done for short bursts of time.

It has always been my belief that any sort of training you can do in the boat is better than any sort you will do on land. If you look at your on-the-water workouts from the standpoint of working muscular strength, or peak strength, it is very hard to find a suitable workout that allows you to fatigue your muscles at such a high level of strain. On the other hand, there are many workouts-whether they be technique, short courses, or sprints-that work your muscles at about 65% of your peak strength in sets of thirty seconds or so. I have found that peak strength is most effectively trained in the gym while muscular endurance is best worked in the boat itself. I just can't believe that weight training is an efficient way to train sports specific muscular endurance when compared to simply working this area on the water.

## Training Peak Strength

I shape my training plan such that it has three distinct phases that take me from fall training through to my spring lactic work. My first phase is a general fitness one. Exercises are non-specific in so far that I do not mimic particular strokes. In this phase I work both muscle groups specific to paddling and muscle groups simply involved in paddling. Lifts are focused specifically on improving my maximum lift strength.

My second phase, which usually follows 8-12 weeks after the initial phase, targets the muscles used for paddling more specifically, i.e. I would use the cable pulls a lot to mimic draws, sweeps, and forward strokes. These workouts actually take the most time since I work so many specific movements on each side. I also focus very specifically on technique in these exercises. This is a great way to develop necessary coordination, especially on complex movements

Photo by Chris Smith.

where the paddler is trying to synchronize his body with his arms while rotating. By using a mirror and working slowly the athlete can focus separately on everything from posture to hand position. Quite often, when training younger or beginning athletes, I have them start these specific exercises in Phase 1 with no weight. This gives them the necessary technique and coordination so that they can begin to build proper strength in Phase 2.

The third phase is a maintenance phase and it simply bridges the gap between gym strength and on-the-water strength. As the paddler begins to transition from his strength and endurance training to specific lactic and speed work they also need to transform their general strength into on-the-water strength, and on-the-water power. To accomplish this paddlers work specific stroke drills in sets designed to train power (unit force/unit time) and finite technique. Strength is also trained by doing short fast courses common to technical workouts. These workouts are far more important to the athlete's overall objectives than any time spent in the gym.

I also include one or two heavy lifts per week into this third phase. One thing we know from tests is that peak strength deteriorates quite quickly if the athlete avoids the gym for any extended period. Time spent in the gym then during this third phase is meant to maintain gym strength without depleting the athlete's strength "battery" enough to affect these more important workouts. Sports docs have found that lifts within 5% of an athlete's maximum are quite effective at maintaining (they do NOT help increase strength) an athlete's gym strength. I call this my maintenance phase and simply do many of the same exercises (not so many specific ones) at a resistance above 95% of my maximum. Keep in mind that this is simply a bridge to fool the body into thinking it has been doing weights much more recently than it has. Later, as the athlete develops their specific strength, and as their priorities focus more on specific race work weights drop out of the

Sports docs have also found that, by basing the amount of weight we lift off of our maximum single rep lift, we can focus on the specific objectives of our training. For example any exertion below about 75% of an athlete's max lift will not increase the athlete's strength but will work an athlete's muscular endurance. In order to target my objective of increasing strength I do all my lifts at 75% of max. or greater.

In general my program consists of 3 sets of lifts per exercise. In the first set I do 10 lifts at 75% of my max weight. For the second set I do 7 lifts at 85% of my max. lift, and for my final set I do 5 reps at 95% of my max lift.

There are two tricks I use to tweak the program a little: I always lift a little heavy so that I can NOT complete the seven and five rep sets. This is because I have read that the lifts that increase your strength are the ones you can't do. Rather I do as many as I can, and then have a spotter nudge the weights along on the remaining lifts.

The second trick I use is to alternate exercises about every five weeks so that I work the same muscles, but from a different angle. So if I was doing pull ups I switch to lat. Pull downs, one arm curls are switched to hammer curls, etc. This is a trick I stole from a book about Olympic Gold Medallist in K-1 flatwater Greg Barton. This workout is featured in Bill Endicott's book, The Barton Mold.

In order to give the workout flow, and to make it go quicker, I alternate between two exercises at a time. This way I am working one thing while resting the other. For example I would do the 75% set at the bench press and then do it at the pull ups before starting the 85% at bench press. This will cut your workout time almost in half. Here is an example of what I would do in each of the three phases:

**Phase 1:**

| Exercise | Approx. Max. lift |
|---|---|
| Bench Press | 250 |
| Pull ups | Bod + 80 lbs. |
| Hammer | Curls 70 |
| Incline Sit ups | Bod + 55 |
| Tricept pull downs | Stack + |
| Pectoral wings | Stack + |
| Seated Row | Stack + |
| Shoulder rolls | 100 lbs (w/good tech) |

**Phase 2:**

| Exercise | Purpose |
|---|---|
| Incline Press | Large involved |
| Lat. Pull down | muscle groups worked |
| | |
| Sit up machine | |
| from a different angle | |
| Chainsaw pulls | Injury rehab and |
| Triceps pull downs | Shoulder rows protection |
| | |
| Shoulder rotations | Draws emphasize |
| Cable pull: | body rotation and |
| | |
| Sweeps | posture. |
| Strokes | Works specific muscles |

**Phase 3:**

I'd vary the angle to the most specific for each exercise. Then I'd do four sets of four lifts at 95% of max. I'd follow that workout with a mid-day workout of stroke drills-for power-on the water.

program in favor of more pressing issues. Typically I am through doing weights about two and a half months before my next big race.

### Training Muscular Endurance

The beauty of training muscular endurance is that you get to do this in the boat. The largest part of your muscular endurance training will come in the form of your technique workouts, since you will need to do these anyway and they already consist of doing 20-30 second bursts. In the fall and winter I also do thirty-second pieces with a funnel on the back of my boat to enhance my muscular endurance training. These sets are done with a heart rate monitor that I use to intentionally keep my heart rate below 160 beats per minute. I do this to avoid going lactic-thus limiting the power of each individual pull-when I am trying to work my strength systems. Usually this means that my stroke rate is quite low, I tend to need to take a break between strokes to keep my pulse low, but each stroke itself is an ultimate effort.

In the winter, starting in January and continuing

through February, and March 1 continue with these technique workouts but also do similar workouts for speed. These "short course" workouts are a hodge-podge of different gate combinations but are done at full speed, usually for time and against some competitors. These runs should be much more intense than your technique workouts and you should feel much more muscular fatigue at the end of the workout. I continue with my funnel work through this period but tend to do less thirty-second paced sets and more ten-second full-speed sprints.

By the time you are into your full time spring training your muscular endurance workouts will be almost entirely short courses and technique. Many paddlers still do sprints through this period but I find I have a hard time fitting this sort of work into a schedule filled with lactic work and race preparation. Be sure to keep a balance between focusing too much on your effort and not enough on your technical priorities, which should still reign supreme in your training.

## Training Power

Training power is different from training strength. Power, in the boat, is the ability to exert force quickly and is often more important to slalom than maximum strength. Developing power is a fickle thing since it must be developed in the same action as it will used. In short, power must also be developed in the boat. I did power workouts in the form of short quick sprints either in a straight line or else through easy offsets. These sprints were ten to twelve seconds long and were done at absolute maximum pace. I found that this sort of training was important year round since it balanced a natural inclination that I had to paddle slowly during the off season.

# Lactic Training

## Physical Objectives of Lactic Training

Not once in my life have I read a discussion on lactic training without feeling I needed a four-year degree in chemistry. This book is meant to be a layman's guide to training and as such you're only going to get the low-down on lactic training. If you want to read about all the chemical reactions buy someone else's book. This is a very basic model on the lactic system which I used in my training.

Your body is an engine. It can run on three different types of fuels. The first is ATP. This is free full-speed energy and it lasts for about seven seconds. You can go as fast and as hard as possible on this juice but it is gone before you know it.

On the other end of the scale your body can burn fat. Exercise that burns fat is called aerobic training. To burn this fat your body requires oxygen and it is the amount of oxygen that you can intake into your blood that limits how much fat you can burn and thus how hard you can train aerobically.

In between these two systems, your short burst ATP and your long slow aerobic, is another system, your lactic system. Basically your lactic system is the system that allows your body to use sugar as a fuel. It is a fantastically efficient system that lets you go really hard until you either run out of sugar (glycogen) or your body clogs up with lactic acid . The sugar (in the form of glycogen) is stored in your muscles and burns without oxygen. You can really cook on this stuff, but you have a limited supply. There's another catch: you can burn yourself out with this stuff. The by-product released when you burn these sugars is called lactic acid. It is a sludge that cramps your arms and makes you burn all over. If you go hard enough for long enough the amount of lactic acid in your blood will inevitably increase until, at a certain point, you will crash and have to stop. Lactic acid is commonly blamed for making your muscles burn with fatigue. It is the combination of running out of glycogen to burn and the build up of lactic acid that cause your body to quickly fatigue and fail when performing at high intensities.

Basically it breaks down like this. They say that about your first seven seconds are fueled by ATP. If you run a hundred-yard dash in ten seconds then

Photo by Chris Smith.

you've spent most of your race in the ATP zone. For about the next two minutes you are in the "lactic-zone," you are running primarily on your sugar supply. Basically a miler spends most of their race relying on sugars as a fuel source. Everything past that point becomes primarily reliant on aerobic systems as a fuel source. Our sport, given that you go for about 120 seconds, is primarily a lactic event. You will have to train your lactic system to its utmost if you want your body to give you its peak performance.

Here's what you need to know: you can train your lactic system in essentially two ways. The first is called peak lactic. This involves starting well rested and going at, or above, race pace for some increment of time. In between each effort you will need to rest at least six times as long as you worked. With this training you are teaching your body to burn more sugar. You are actually teaching your body to give you its most efficient peak output. In a strictly phys-

Photo by Chris Smith.

ical sense the goal of this workout is to teach your body to efficiently burn glycogen and to deal with the pain associated with lactic buildup.

The second type of lactic training is called lactic tolerance. The objective of these workouts is to train your body to deal with that lactic acid and still perform at a high level. These workouts are done at a high pace (race pace or above) but with little rest between efforts. Essentially you are raising the lactic acid levels in your blood up to a relatively high level and then maintaining that level while still demanding coordinated performance from your body. These are very painful workouts. Lactic tolerance workouts usually last as long as you can take them.

## Technical Objectives of Lactic Training

Peak Lactic: Your peak lactic workouts are the closest thing you will have to a real race in your entire training program. These workouts should be your most important workouts. You should do whatever you can to improve both the quality of this workout and the amount you prepare for it. Your objective-you want to create a workout that is as similar to a real race situation as possible and then you want to win this workout. You will find that the workout has little value unless you spend a lot of time preparing off the water for the time you will spend on the water. This means that you need to take the time to set a high quality course (correct pole heights, number of gates, and difficulty of moves) that is unfamiliar to you.

I cannot emphasize enough that the course should be unfamiliar to you. Try to set moves that you have not done before. If you are having trouble imagining what these moves might be have someone else design the course for you, in particular use someone who is not familiar with your training site.

I also cannot emphasize enough how much having a quality course matters. Your training will do you very little good if you have high poles, not enough gates or moves that are easy or standard to your training. I used to train with a club in North Carolina who were often slack in this respect. On one especially slack phase of training I went away for a month to train in Costa Rica and came back to find the gates in BOTH their slalom courses still in the same place I left them!

It is also very important that you use your peak lactic workouts to practice your mental preparation for racing. Five-Time World Champion Richard Fox wrote in his training log that he would set aside at least three workouts a week where he would fully mentally prepare for his runs. This means walking the course and putting together a race plan. This means fully visualizing the course from top to bottom the way you would in a race. Finally, it means that after each run you need to evaluate that run both technically, in terms of how well you executed your plan, and analytically in terms of how well your plan worked. On each run you should refine and refine your plan until, by the end of the workout, you are not only executing the moves perfectly, but also executing the perfect course.

### Try this workout:

#### Workout: Mock Race, 2 x full lengths

Type: Peak Lactic

Protocol: This workout should be no different than the most intense race you do all season. If you can, set the course and prepare for the race the night before, just as you'd do in an actual race. For races I usually do a double warm-up, so I do the same thing for this workout, paddling about two hours before I start for the race. Also be sure to make your entire day leading up to the race the same as game day. I like to set start times in advance with at least an hour between runs to more closely mimic a true race.

Intensity: Do these at race pace, period. Be sure to have at least an hour's rest between runs.

An important part of this workout is the debriefing after you have finished. I like to sit down with a piece of paper (my training log), and go through all the mistakes I made throughout the workout. Was I hungry but forgot food? Did I feel warmed-up enough at the start? Was I late for my start? This workout should serve two purposes: it should get you ready to race and perform at a high level when it really counts, but it should also be a dry run of an important race day where you can sort out the particulars of being ready.

There are also some exceptional workouts that require an extra amount of attention. As you lead into your most important race you should begin to practice actually doing that race. We call these dry runs "Mock Races," and they should mimic the actual race in every way possible. For my first few team selection races I would do these Mock Races at the actual racecourse. I would stay in the same hotel, get up at the same time, do a double warm-up and everything else associated with that race. These are a fantastic way to find potential problems with your race day routine. Sometimes I would actually sit down the night after these workouts and fill out a page with things to remember for the upcoming selection race.

**Lactic Tolerance:** Lactic Tolerance workouts have a considerably different agenda than the peak lactic workouts. The lactic tolerance workouts are more about wearing yourself out more and more while still trying to paddle at a your maximum pace. Where the peak lactic workouts were about getting the utmost in quality by resting and preparing, the lactic tolerance is all about maintaining what quality you can while depriving yourself of much needed rest and recovery. The format of these workouts usually involves doing a course between thirty seconds and a minute with between a half to a quarter of that time spent as rest.

There is a catch though. You must always paddle at your maximum level. There is no pacing in these workouts, you are simply going as hard as you possibly can and fading throughout each piece. This means you will get tired and your quality will tend to fade. Since your courses aren't very technical you should be doing some fairly standard maneuvers. Your objective is to maintain your good technique in the face of all the pain you will be feeling, and to continue to keep your boat on line.

# Aerobic Training

## Physical Objectives of Aerobic Training

Aerobic training is the cornerstone of a slalom paddler's fitness. Most coaches consider an athlete's aerobic fitness to be the basis upon which the rest of their training rests. Virtually every successful yearly training plan will start with three or four months that are split between improving an athlete's general strength and improving their general fitness. The idea is that the athlete will use their improved strength to develop power when the season rolls around and likewise will use their aerobic fitness to develop their lactic system.

Perhaps the easiest model to think of is a big wide flat base that is your aerobic and strength training. Upon this base you will put a narrower second level that is your white-hot lactic system. It uses your aerobically fit body as an engine, but uses its white-hot sugar fuel system to launch you our of plodding work mode into your lightning quick mode. Onto this narrower level is a narrower level still that is your power. You should train your power at the same time you train your lactic system so that your racehorse will have horsepower. You need this power to give your newfound quickness a spring to its step.

Your race run will be filled with instances when you need to leap ahead either to get the boat moving or else to sprint the boat through a certain gate combination. Much of this discussion should be saved for the section on how to put together a yearly plan, but the thing to keep in mind is this: your fitness pyramid can only be as wide as the lowest level. You cannot build a superior lactic system on an inferior aerobic system. Essentially how fit you are able to be in the spring will be based on the amount of basic fitness you do in the fall. This is why aerobic training is often considered to be "training so you can train."

Physically, aerobic training does a lot of things. It will increase your blood volume, which increases the amount of oxygen your body can transport to your muscles. It will increase the number of capillaries in your muscles that transport blood, thereby making it easier for that oxygen rich blood to feed you muscles. In short, you will be training your entire cardio-respiratory system to consume, absorb, transport, and efficiently utilize more oxygen

There are two general types of aerobic training that

Photo by Chris Smith.

we do for whitewater slalom. The first, long aerobic training, does essentially all of the above things. Long endurance workouts help create a body that is capable of sustained periods of high intensity training. You are training your body so that it will be fit for more intense workouts later; training so that you can train. This long endurance training usually takes the form of long non-stop paddling at a medium-hard endurance pace. If you have access to testing equipment and heart rate monitors, this pace will correspond to training below about 4 millimoles of blood lactate. For those of us who don't have access to such testing (count me in!), go at a pace that you can maintain for long periods of time, say forty minutes or so. This pace should be hard enough that you cannot carry on any sort of a reasonable conversation without getting completely out of breath. This pace should be, as Olympic gold medallist Greg Barton would say, just outside the comfort zone. Long

Photo by Chris Smith.

endurance workouts can be either straight-ahead across flatwater, or in gates. I tend to find that a hybrid works best. I do many of these workouts as a loop through gates with approximately an extra two minutes per lap added on as straight ahead distance.

The second general type of aerobic training we do in slalom is called Lactic-Endurance. These are workouts where you are training your body to perform at or above your anaerobic threshold. It works like this: the harder you train the higher your pulse-rate will climb. This is your body's natural reaction to increased exertion. It is your body's attempt to supply oxygen to your muscles so that they can burn fat for energy.

At some point, gradually at first, your body will need to start burning sugar to keep up with your demand for energy. The aerobic system simply cannot supply energy at the rate you are demanding it. The harder you go the more your body will need to use this energy source.

Unfortunately, you are up against an exponentially increasing curve where each increment of increased effort will correspond to a massive increase in sugar burned and lactic acid produced. This is where the idea of an anaerobic threshold comes in.

For each of us there is a point up to which we are quite able to increase our intensity. Once we cross this point, like stepping off a cliff, our lactic levels begin to spiral and we will find ourselves quickly in need of rest. This point is called the anaerobic threshold and much of your training will be dedicated to raising this point to its highest possible level. This is called threshold training.

Threshold training, or as I call it "lactic-endurance," usually involves training either right at, or above and below, your lactic threshold. Some of the workouts simply involve going at or above your threshold for an extended period of time, say five minutes for example. You would then rest long enough for your pulse to recover to a reasonable rate, in this case for one to two minutes, before doing another piece of the same length.

The second type of lactic-endurance workouts are the, and I'm using the name liberally here, "Fartlek" workouts. These are named after the guy who invented a type of threshold training that involves "active recovery." This type of training is done without ever truly taking a rest during an active set. The athlete alternates between pieces of a shorter length that are done at an intensity higher than your threshold and pieces of a longer length that are done below your threshold. I usually think of these two paces in this sense. I do the harder segments at about race pace-the rate at which I would race-and for the easier segments work just a little too hard to carry on a conversation.

Often, depending on the intensity of the "On-time," I will make the recovery time quite long to allow for a complete active recovery before I begin the next repetition.

## Try this workout:

### Workout: 30 minute "paddle about"

Type: Long Endurance

Protocol: Spend thirty or more minutes paddling through gates on easy moving or flat water.

Intensity: Very low, this workout should feel like all you did was warm up for a little more than a half hour or so.

I worked with a British coach who loved to do lactic work- and loved to do this workout. This is a great recovery from the lactic stuff and a great way to focus only on precision and gate execution. Typically I don't even set a course for this workout. Instead I make courses as I go, usually working on whatever I feel needs the most help at the time. I also use this workout as a low intensity way to work problems in your technique without the pressure of a coach watching, or a watch timing.

## Technical Objectives of Aerobic Training

Most of the gates you do, most of the strokes you take and most of your time spent paddling your boat will be done in endurance workouts. There has been some research to support that endurance workouts, due to their repetitive nature, are a fantastic way to learn technique. This means that if you do your long endurance with good technique you will go a long way towards making your good intentions into good habits.

There is a flip side however: If you practice bad technique through these workouts you will find you have made bad technique a habit. Your objective should be to make all of your endurance workouts deliberate and concise. The best paddlers, even in the painful throws of fatigue, force themselves to two-stroke the upstreams and peg all the offsets.

A great example of this is one of my favorite workouts. I often go for a couple of thirty-minute easy gate loops to help me recover from all the lactic sessions from the week. Physically this has a recovery effect which helps clean out all the sludge in my cramped up muscles. These workouts rarely involve a set course and I simply paddle up to the top of the training gates and then back through them at my easiest endurance pace. When I actually negotiate a gate though, whether it be a down or an upstream gate, I peg that gate perfectly and powerfully. Every upstream is done in two strokes and I am prepared for every offset, which I snap through. This is a fantastic workout because it prioritizes technique above all else while still having the desired physical effect for my training.

# The Yearly Training Plan

Figuring out when to put which workouts where is often a difficult task. Many paddlers ignore making a yearly plan and simply do either what the coaches ask or else just do whatever comes to mind when they get on the water. Remember, there is an easy way to get fast and a hard way, simply doing random workouts is one of the hardest ways. Your body needs certain types of workouts to learn the skills of paddling and certain types of workouts to gain the fitness needed to paddle fast for the length of a slalom course. How you put these workouts together can mean the difference between being tired and training ineffectively all year and being a shooting star that repeatedly has great workouts.

The most important thing to remember is that you are not only scheduling your work, you are scheduling your rest. One of my favorite quotes on this subject comes from Alexander Pope though he was actually discussing music at the time. He would ask his students to bang and bang on a piano such that it constantly made noise. Then he would ask them if all that noise made music. His point, in his own words, was this, "The silence is as important as the sound," music is the orchestration of the right sounds with the right amount of silence.

Training is the same way. Your body works on a cycle of stimulus and response. If you simply tear the muscles up continually without letting them recover, you will never get stronger since it is the rebuilding of muscle fiber that actually makes you stronger. This phenomenon of training so much that your body cannot adequately recover is called over-training and is prevalent in virtually all sports. You could safely say that every athlete has, at one time or another, over-trained. In fact, athletes training for World and Olympic medals will need to skirt the edge of over-training for virtually the entire year in order to be prepared for those events. The problem is that an over-trained athlete is much more susceptible to sickness, injury, and fatigue. In the case of our sport they are also often too tired to maintain good technique or to work at the proper intensity needed for many workouts.

Sports science has been searching for a way to detect over-training in an athlete for years. There are several tests, such as resting heart-rate or blood chemistry analysis that have been marginally successful predictors of over-training, but none that I believe truly predicts it. I have found a way to avoid the issue entirely by taking control of my training cycles. This actually allows me to over-train at the peak of a training cycle, but then completely recover from my training before I reach a stage where I am in danger of serious injury or sickness. Here's the kicker to the whole thing: It is the best way to train for a technical sport like whitewater slalom and... the sports scientists, who call this cyclic training "periodization", believe that it is the fastest way to gain fitness. You couldn't hope for a better combination of reasons to train this way.

Periodization is a way to cycle your training to ensure that you are getting enough training and enough rest. Here's how it works. First, you divide your year up into larger macro-cycles. Within each macro-cycle you schedule smaller cycles called micro-cycles. These micro-cycles will vary in overall difficulty (a combination of volume and intensity) such that some weeks are harder and some weeks are easier than your average training week. The net sum of a macro-cycle though is that you have completed a full circle of training your body to ultimate fatigue and then returning it to complete rest. Each cycle should begin fresh from ground zero. This way your over-training is limited to the length of a cycle minus the time it took you to recover from your training. Most often this precluded wearing myself out to the point of exhaustion that might have lead to illness and injury.

I divide my training up into macro-cycles of four weeks. This has several advantages. Your training should change throughout the year. For example, fall

training cycles typically have more endurance workouts than spring training cycles. By compartmentalizing my training I am able to assign priorities, both physical and technical, to each cycle. Macro-cycles gave a logical start and end to these seasonal goals. The physical advantage to working this way is two-fold. First off, each compartment is a completely separate entity. When I finish one cycle I'm rested and ready to begin another cycle-regardless of what that cycle focuses on. The other advantage is that I shape my training in a stair-step fashion.

Stair-step training is also known as periodization. It involves training separate weeks differently, some of them harder and some of them easier. Think of the fitness you would gain from the steady state training you are doing now. Each week is probably pretty similar to the previous one in volume and number of rest workouts. This would give you a fitness curve that would steadily improve making you fitter and fitter the longer you continued to train.

Now imagine a training plan where you worked harder some weeks and easier some weeks. The net amount of training will average out to be the same amount of time per week but, because your body responds better to being over-worked and then adequately rested, you will gain fitness faster than a steady state trainer.

There's actually a fantastic technical reason why I've latched onto this training regime so tightly. When I was first training there were two top paddlers in my training group. One was Rich Weiss, many time U.S. National Champion and World Medallist. The other was Patrice Gagnon, many-time Canadian National champion and a constant resident of the World's top ten. Having these two training in the same place made for a tremendous contrast in training methodology. Rich was a workhorse, not that Rich had poor technique or poor training habits, but he could work harder and better than any man who ever paddled slalom. Rich constantly trained thirteen workouts a week or more. However, Rich rarely took a rest from this regime. Rich himself called this type of training "scattershot" training. He figured that if you simply did enough workouts some of them would be good and that was where you would make your technical improvements.

Patrice was just the opposite. By Rich's standard you might have considered him to be a bit of a slacker. In fact, he was quite the opposite. Patrice was one of the most thorough athletes in our sport. He would train whitewater about six times a week but his training was very different from the sorts of workouts Rich and I would do. Patrice would arrive early and with a mission in mind. His goal for the workout might be offsets for example. Before getting on the water he would position all the gates such that he had a perfect offset course for what he wanted to work on. His workout would then consist of systematically working those offsets until he had perfected the skill he had set out to master. Each workout he did on whitewater was done with adequate rest, good

Photo by Chris Smith.

planning and organization, and precise execution. Rarely would he be too tired maintain good technique or too rushed to jump on the water without the ideal training situation being set.

The net result was interesting. At their peak you would have needed a watch to separate Rich and Patrice's times. It was fascinating to me that they had arrived there by such different paths. What I was looking for even before I learned about periodization was a way to blend these two systems of training. Periodization is ideal for this. Cyclic training allows for periods of heavy training and periods where you are more recovered, more able to rest before your workouts. The combination gives you the fitness of intense training along with the quality of not-so-intense training.

In 1993 I visited the Olympic Training Center in Colorado Springs, Colorado with the U.S. Team. By this point in time I had been using my own version of periodization for quite some time in my training. What the sports scientists at the USOC convinced me to do was alter this schedule such that I steadily increased my volume and intensity over a three-week period and then resting the fourth. This was the "textbook" method of periodizing training at the time. What I found was that this may be ideal for athletes in less technical sports but is less than ideal for slalom. Such a long building phase will put you below peak performance somewhere in the middle of the first week and leave you there for the next two weeks. Three weeks of steadily increasing your workload quickly leads to poor quality training. For half the month you will be paddling when you are too tired to maintain good technique. Instead I have developed a system where I rotate my training week-by-week.

My first week is hard. I think of it as being just a little more than what an average training week would be. By the end of this week I am just beginning to be to tired too train effectively in the harder workouts. After a short break, usually a day with one recovery workout, I begin a medium week. This week is usually just below the average training load and is usually easy enough that I am recovered and training effectively by Sunday. The third week is then super-hard. This week, in volume and intensity, is the utmost I can do and still continue to train. I like to think of the last three days of this week as "borrowed time"-as I continue to train past this point I am no longer able to recover in a single day. This is self-induced over-training! The fourth week is a complete recovery. I tend to take a couple of days off and then spend the rest of the week doing recovery endurance and focused technique sessions. This recovery week prepares me for whatever the next macro-cycle may bring.

## Making a yearly plan

I always thought that putting together a yearly plan was the most important off-the-water task I set for myself each year. In fact, I felt like it wasn't enough to just have that plan. I felt like you yourself had to take part in creating it. Your yearly plan dictates your technical and physical priorities for each of you training cycles. Without having a yearly plan to guide you it would be virtually impossible to set your weekly training schedules. Without this yearly plan you are like a person lost in a maze that constantly takes each turn because it looks more appealing than another choice. A yearly plan is the roadmap that ensures you will start your training in the fall and arrive at the World Championships the next summer in peak condition. I have always done my own yearly plan since I believe that this gives you the knowledge you need to train effectively.

It is important before you start that you completely understand your purpose in the task ahead of you. You are responsible for making sure that, on the morning of race day, you are the fastest person you can be. That is your overriding goal. Doing this involves preparing for every aspect of the race day ahead of you, not just being the fittest person you can be. Putting together a yearly plan allows you to over-lay your preparations for all the aspects of training so that you are completely prepared, technically, mentally, logistically, and physically.

The previous section discussed a little of the science involved in physically and technically training your body to race. Inherent in even that simple discussion are many different variables which affect your training and which somehow must be incorporated into your training. There are many different methods in which this can be done and many other books which delve into this topic more completely than I do. This, however, is a practical book. This is how we train today. What follows is a case study of how I put together my training year from the first workout in the fall to the start of my most important race of the year.

**Step 1:** Take the time to set some reasonable goals for your year's training and write them down. I don't mean goals like, "I will be World Champion with only a year's training," but goals like, "I will be at such-and-such a level by next year and to do this I need to achieve this or that by the time next season rolls around." What you are trying to do is set a standard of achievement by next year. Whether that standard is World Champion, or National Team Member, or winning the novice class at a local race does not matter. You are trying to decide where you would like to be at the end of your training season, and what sort of things you need to accomplish to get to that point. You are setting goals that will get you to where you want to be next season. You should also take an honest look at what is involved in achieving those goals and decide whether you are prepared to make that commitment. If you wrote down that you will be a World Champion by next year you had better be prepared to put everything you have into training between now and the next championships. A more realistic goal such as being the fastest in your region might fit better into a busy work and family life.

**Step 2:** Plot, either in your mind or on paper, a route to your destination. If, for example, you wrote "Olympic Champion" as your goal then in your mind

look at what you would need to do to surpass the efforts of the current world number one. Upcoming talents are the most guilty of making this mistake. Nineteen year olds often have trouble leaving the junior ranks because they, in their first year of college, often train harder than they have ever trained and still miss the transition from Junior team member to senior team member.

Remember, you are not simply training for a personal best! You must train BETTER than your competition if you want to beat them! This is true at whichever level you choose to train. If you want to be the best in your region, you must train better than anyone in your region. If you want to be the best in the Country you had better train better than the best in the country, regardless of how much you have trained in the past.

**Step 3:** Now that you have some idea of the scope of your task, it is time to break this down into simple manageable steps. Set some very general technical goals for yourself. These can be such things as improving your cleanliness in gates, or learning to do upstreams in two strokes, or learning to race better. Make a list of all of these things (hint: your list should have all three of those on it, regardless of your ability). Keep in mind both your own ability and how much you must improve to reach your goal. For example, if you are shooting for a spot on a National team you should be very adept at two stroke upstreams.

**Step 4:** Map out your entire year in big squares on big pieces of paper. You should have a box big enough for writing comments for each week of your training year. I like to number the boxes in reverse, from "week 1"-the week of the big race-back to the week I began my training. For the 2000 Olympic trials I began preparing at "week 24". This should lay out your entire year of training in one big timeline style calendar.

The trick now is to fit together all of your training objectives, both technical and physical, into those squares such that you are ready to race by the end of "week 1."

**Step 5:** Let's put the easy ones in first, these are the standard things every top athlete needs in order to be successful on the day of competition.

## Phase One

Set aside five weeks for final race preparation: I will write more about this final five weeks later in this section, but for now pencil this area in as off-limits to other objectives. Lots of athletes and coaches continue their normal training plan right up to within a couple of weeks of the big event. I try to be completely ready to race at this five-week point. This does a couple of things, it gives me a heads-up about any problems I am having while I still have five-weeks to fix them and it gives me five-weeks of training at or near race-pace. Training plans that prepare your lactic system and race technique for just the last week before the race are prone to all sorts of problems from the standpoints both of being physically prepared and being technically ready to race.

Circle that day five weeks before the race : This is your test day. Your yearly training plan should, in many ways, prepare you for this day. The last five weeks will simply hone the ability you have on this day. Do either a real or mock race at some point in the later part of this week. Take the time to evaluate the way you raced, the energy you had, your pace, everything you can think of that had to do with your performance. You will take these problems to task in those last five weeks.

Group your remaining weeks into four-week macro-cycles: Count your macro-cycles out backwards from this five-week point. Whether your training starts in the middle of a macro-cycle is unimportant as long as you completely finish and recover from a macro-cycle before you reach the five-week point. Label each week in your macro-cycles in order as Hard, Medium, Super-Hard, and Easy. If you are not a full-time athlete you may find that this four-week system is cumbersome and interrupts your work or family life. Instead, try using a two-week cycle that is merely a hard week followed by an easy one. This should be easier to manage.

## Phase Two

Set aside six to eight weeks for lactic training: Your lactic system takes six to eight weeks to train. This is a system that you simply must prepare if you want to race effectively. You should set aside this much time regardless of how little or much time you have till your big event. If you only have seven or eight weeks between when you start training for the year and the day of your big event, then start training your lactic system. I tend to train this system for about four weeks before I reach the five-week point. This way my lactic system is mostly prepared for my test day and I can evaluate how much lactic work I'll need in the last few weeks.

Circle the start of lactic training and write CLEANLI-NESS!: The start of lactic training signals the beginnings of getting ready to race. Now is the time to start forcing yourself to be clean. U.S. Team Coach Bill Endicott estimates that top athletes are clean on 80-90% of the runs that they do!

## Phase Three

Set aside eight weeks to transition your training from aerobic to lactic: Your training before this transition phase will consist of a balance between your long aerobic work and your short technical work. I like to set aside two macro-cycles where I add in a lot of lactic-endurance workouts to begin working my body at a more intense pace. These shorter pieces allow me to get used to pushing myself while still working my endurance. This is often the hardest and highest volume part of my year. I also tend to begin doing full-length race practice in this time period. Mostly this is just to get myself tuned back into the feel of a full-length race run.

## Phase Four

Set aside the rest of your training for aerobic and technical training: The best thing you can do before

phase three starts is work on developing physically by getting stronger and fitter and working on your technique. These early workouts are a great time to work on whitewater skills and stroke basics as well as mastering new techniques on the slalom course.

Now you see why putting together a training plan is so much easier than you thought. The structure is already there! What you have created now is a template for success that virtually any athlete could use to prepare for the upcoming season. For the most part you have now finished planning the physical part of your year's training. The tricky part is tailoring this to fit your needs. These are the strategies I use to weave other aspects of my training in with the physical plan:

**Technical Objectives:** Every year should have its own technical objectives. It is not enough to say that you want to be better at the same stuff next year than you were this year. You must evaluate your previous year's results and decide EXACTLY which things need improving before next season and then make a point of improving them. If you had difficulty with hard moves, or offsets, or lost time in upstreams last year then you need to make a point of not only improving them, but practicing them, re-evaluating yourself, and practicing them some more. The best way to ensure that this happens is to decide what those things are now, and write down a time by which you will have improved this skill.

I find that phase four is the best time to experiment and make changes to my technique. I actually set a self-coached training camp every fall with the express purpose of breaking down every aspect of my technique, evaluating it, and then deciding what I will spend the fall working on. In your yearly plan write in what sorts of technical things you would like to prioritize over which time periods. If you are training year round you will typically have eight to ten weeks with which to play with new technique in your technical sessions and then practice them in your endurance workouts.

I also find that it is important to write, or circle, a date at which you want to be through with experimenting with new things and begin to solidify the techniques you want to use for next year. This doesn't mean stop learning new things altogetherIt means that from this point on you will begin to focus on honing the techniques you have learned. By circling this day you also have a set point in time where you should sit down and evaluate your progress. Having checkpoints throughout the year ensures that you don't wake up one day in the spring and realize you should have worked on something months ago. If you feel that you need to work a little more on something, now is the time to make that happen while you are still months from the big event.

Phase Three of your training should hone your skills to the point where you can consistently repeat your performances time after time. Phase three involves a heavy workload with lots of intense endurance that can lead to bad habits and inconsistent runs. Forcing yourself to keep your form through this phase is one of the best ways to ensure consistent runs next spring.

Phase Two is really the final phase of your technical development for the year. In phase two you should be, during your lactic training, practicing using your new technique in race situations. This is also a good time to evaluate how well your changes survive the test under fire.

Unfortunately, not all things can fit into this mold. A lot of the skills involved in racing can't be practiced in the fall when you aren't supposed to be training your lactic system very much. Practicing racing involves mastering a bunch of different skills that are both physical and mental. Some of these skills such as visualization and difficult moves can be practiced in the fall by working them into your technique and endurance workouts. Others, like full-length runs or mock races are best worked as you come closer to the time when you will train your lactic system.

In my training I would start doing a small number of full length race runs during phase three to work on the skill of putting together a "full length" itself. Often these early full-length workouts would be tweaked to work a particular skill such as pace or consistency rather than simply trying to bang out race runs one after the other. Another athlete who hasn't had as much experience racing might decide to do full-length practice throughout the year. Take the time now to decide exactly what skills you would like to work and then decide for yourself where and when they fit into your year.

**CREATE YOUR OWN TRAINING CAMPS:** Training camps are a great way to force yourself to put aside everything else and focus on your training. I tend to set aside two or three weeks a year as "un-coached camps." I format these camps the same way they would be if you were visiting a coach who was setting the schedule for you. The first camp I do is in the fall and I spend the entire camp (about four days) learning just basic technique. I completely take apart the way I've been paddling and re-learn everything from strokes to basic upstreams and offsets. A lot of times I'll compare the way I'm doing these maneuvers with the way others are doing them to decide which ones I like best. This way I spend the long hours of fall training working on specifically the technique I'd like to use the following year.

My second camp usually falls right before the start of phase two. I like to take a week in here and practice racing. I'll spend four to six days at a whitewater training site doing full-lengths, half-lengths, speed courses; the whole nine yards just like I would do in the spring. This way I can practice the skills of racing long before it really matters to decide what sorts of things I'll need to work on. This is also a fun way to spend your Christmas break.

Typically my last camp would be somewhere before the start of my five-week phase. This one I would actually do with other team members or international competitors. This camp is non-stop competition. I continually try and pick either races or workouts with the fastest people I can find to hone my skills for the summer. Don't let yourself become discouraged by your relative results. It is often true that you'll lose

these workouts to others. Dig in and try and beat them at any cost! Staying late and doing extra runs to kick ass is allowed.

## WEEKLY PLANS

Once you've set aside time for your training camps and filled in your technical goals, you should have a pretty good idea what sort of year you're going to have. The hard part for you now will be trying to figure out how to use this yearly guide to set your day-to-day workouts. Setting your weekly schedules, which I think of as "micro-cycles," takes a little practice and getting used to. Often the schedule you write for a particular week will be either too hard or too easy and you'll find that you need to adjust it for the next micro-cycle. In my training I find that even though I write my daily plans at the start of each four-week macro-cycle I tend to change them again and again at the start of each week. Don't be afraid

Photo by Chris Smith.

to be dynamic, your macro-cycle is meant to be a guide to your training. Your micro-cycles are meant to tailor your training to your personal needs.

Your individual weeks will also "cycle" the way your larger training cycles do. The trick to putting together an effective training week is "rotating" your workouts so that the workouts complement each other. This way you can use some workouts to help you recover from others.

Remember to use your yearly plan to help you set your weekly priorities. Typically I set my week up as a cycle where I stress the most important physical system and let it recover while I do workouts that maintain the other systems that aren't as important at the time. In this way I am recovered and ready to give my all when I do the important workouts. The less important workouts can be fit in between these important "pillars" of your training week.

I get my weekly priorities from my yearly plan. For example, in the fall I would have long endurance, muscular strength and fitness as my primary physical priorities. Technically I would spend the fall focusing on learning new technique. These workouts would then become the "must-do" workouts for my week. In the fall I would also maintain a few things to be worked enough to maintain my current ability, but not enough to really expect any improvements in these areas. My week in the fall might include these workouts (look in the workouts section to find descriptions of these workouts):

### PRIORITIES
Long-Endurance:
  5 x 9' hard, 3' med.
  60' distance on flatwater
  90' distance on flatwater
  2 x 8(45"on, 2:15 med.)
Technique: Focused technique (three or four times that week)
Strength: Weights (three times that week)

### IMPORTANT
Fitness: Run (twice that week)

### MAINTENANCE
Speed work: 20 x (10" sprints per week)

Those workouts that are a priority are then given the choicest position for the week. I am careful to put at least a day between key workouts so that I am able to rest that particular system and prepare it for another quality workout. In this case I might put the three weight workouts on Monday, Wednesday, and Friday. Since I have the best opportunity to paddle on whitewater on weekends I want to make sure I make the best of these two days.

From the start I'll pencil in two of the technique workouts for Saturday and Sunday morning. I'll also put the 2 x 8(45"on, 2'15 med) on the weekend since this is a great long endurance workout to do on whitewater.

Now I go back and fill in the rest of the week with the remaining workouts. The important thing to remember is to CYCLE. I would essentially try and wear my body down, give it a little recovery, and then wear it down again. For example I would do the weights Monday morning and a technique workout Monday afternoon while I was still fresh. Tuesday morning I might start again with a hard workout, like 5(9'on, 3'med) but then would give my upper body a

rest by going for a run Tuesday afternoon. Wednesday would start the cycle again with the weights followed by a 90' paddle that afternoon, making Wednesday a pretty hard day. Thursday would be easier with just a technique workout and a run in the afternoon.

Look at the entire week and see how it makes three distinct cycles of work and then recovery. Also notice how I leave the week's only complete rest till just before the weekend thus ensuring I will be recovered for the important whitewater workouts.

The winter schedule is usually the hardest in a physical sense. I tend to prioritize the lactic-endurance while still working the long endurance quite hard. For me this is the most demanding season of the year and I tend to work myself to exhaustion on an almost daily basis. Here is an example of how I put together a winter schedule (look in the workouts section to find descriptions of these workouts).

### PRIORITIES
Lactic Endurance
  2 x 20' P.E.
  Prono Loops
  10(3' on, 1' off)
Strength: Weights (three times that week)
Technique:
  Focused technique x 2
  Short Shorts

### MAINTENANCE
Lactic-Endurance
  10 x 3 min. Loops
Long-Endurance
  3 x 15' paddle about
  2 x 20' F.W. Distance
Fitness
  2 x 30' run

A spring schedule might be a lot different. In the spring I'd focus much more on specific race and whitewater work. I would emphasize full-length workouts and speed/technique workouts in order to train my lactic system and prepare for paddling at top speed in big whitewater. My endurance work would be put on maintenance although I would continue to work a little on shorter lactic-endurance workouts and would use the long slow endurance to recover from some of the harder lactic workouts.

## Fall Schedule

|  | Monday | Tuesday | Wednesday | Thursday | Friday | Saturday | Sunday |
|---|---|---|---|---|---|---|---|
| A.M. | Weights | 5(9'on, 3'med) Flatwater Distance | Weights | Technique + 5(10" sprints) | Weights | Technique + 5(10" sprints) | Technique + 5(10" sprints) |
| P.M. | Technique + 5(10" sprints) | 40' Run | 90' Flatwater Distance | 40' Run | — | 2 x 8(45"on, 2'15 Med) Gate Endurance on Whitewater | 90' Flatwater Distance |

# Winter Schedule

|  | Monday | Tuesday | Wednesday | Thursday | Friday | Saturday | Sunday |
|---|---|---|---|---|---|---|---|
| **A.M.** | 2 x 20' P.E. | Focused Technique | Weights | 2 x 20' Flatwater Distance | Prono Loops | Fulls x 5 | 10(3' on, 1' off) |
| **P.M.** | Weights | 30' Run | 3 x 15' Gate Loops | Short Shorts | 30' Run | Weights | Technique |

Here is an example of how I put together a spring schedule (look in the workouts section to find descriptions of these workouts).

## PRIORITIES
Lactic Endurance
       Full lengths-Mock Race + two runs
       Half -lengths
       60's-3 courses, 3 times each

Lactic Tolerance:
       Berger Loops
       Technique/ shorts
       5 x 5 short courses
       Focused Technique
       World Cup Shorts
       Short sprint shorts

## MAINTENANCE
Lactic-Endurance
       10 x 3 min. Loops
Long-Endurance
       3 x 15' paddle about
       2 x 20' F.W. Distance
Fitness 2 x 30' run

This would be a fairly typical spring schedule for me. Notice again how each lactic workout gets a priority slot in the week by being led by a recovery workout. This is to ensure that the paddler is fresh and rested for these fast workouts. This schedule also focuses on the technical with four different short course workouts. Notice also how the harder lactic endurance and the long endurance are simply maintained with only two workouts each a week. These endurance workouts are placed such that the lactic-endurance workouts do not affect the important lactic workouts while the long endurance workouts actually help to recover from the lactic.

# Race Prep: The Final Five Weeks

I have almost always used a five-week model when preparing for races. It creates a mark in the sand that serves both as a heads up for the upcoming race and a starting place for your final race preparation. Technically you should use this five-week point to completely evaluate your paddling and decide what it is that you need to focus on as you begin your last few weeks of training. Physically you should be ready to train one last hard cycle so that you come into the race in the best possible physical condition.

## The Five Week Point

The five-week point is key to my race preparation. The five-week point is exactly what its name implies. It is simply the day that is five weeks before your next big event. I have found that I race best if I actually train to be ready for this point. Let me say this again. I shape my training so that I am completely prepared to race at a point five weeks BEFORE THE RACE!

This does a lot of things. For one it allows you to evaluate how you will perform at top speed and to evaluate if you are on track to have a fully prepared lactic system for the race. You can test all these things while you still have five weeks to make some adjustments. This is also a great way to ensure that you don't peak a week after the race.

The idea is that this five-week point does several things: first off it gives you a chance to evaluate your state of readiness for the upcoming event. Secondly, in preparing for this five-week point you

# Spring Schedule

|  | Monday | Tuesday | Wednesday | Thursday | Friday | Saturday | Sunday |
|---|---|---|---|---|---|---|---|
| **A.M.** | 60's (3 x 3 courses) | 5 x 5 Short courses | 1/2 Lengths x 7 | 10(3' on, 1' off) Flatwater Distance | Prono Loops | Fulls Mock Race + 2 runs | Berger Loops (2 sets) |
| **P.M.** | 3 x 15' "Paddle About" | 30' Run | Technique (focus on jumping Drops) | World Cup Shorts | Rest | Short Shorts | 30' Run |

completely rest your body. Doing this gives you some time to become familiar again with how it feels to paddle in top form again.

In an alternate model that I see many of my competitors using, you can train to peak just for the race. My experience with preparing just in time for the race is that you end up getting only a week or so worth of racing at your top speed. This is something you could have a lot of trouble with on race day.

Think about what this means technically. You would have practiced paddling at the pace you will race at for only seven or so days before the race! For me this has led to mistakes and a general feeling that gates are coming at me far too quickly. If your lactic system is trained and you are ready to race five weeks before the race then you can put together a final race preparation that gives you five times more practice at race pace than a peak-for-the-race approach.

The most important part of my race preparation is to force myself to come to a complete rest three

Photo by Chris Smith.

times in the last five weeks. The first of these is leading into the five weeks. I take a break in week six to rest up for week five, which you'll see is a very difficult week. This break zero's the scale so that you are familiar with what complete rest feels like, which is super important, and so that you are completely prepared to begin a heavy training cycle.

The second rest point is at the end of week two and the final is for the race. Do not underestimate the value of being completely rested at these key points in time. This whole five-week plan is based as much on the rest periods as it is on the training periods. Remember that the silence is as important as the sound.

The idea behind using a five-week cycle is that you are taking control of your training far in advance of the race. This way you can insure that your rest and your training are ideal for the last five weeks. Use these tips as a roadmap to help you plan your final five weeks:

## Week5

Week 5 is the loading phase and actually stretches into week four. Typically I stretch this week out a little extra so that it is ten days of hard work and not just seven. In this phase I'm looking to train my body to the very brink of exhaustion. I normally add just a little to my most intense week (keep in mind we're training lactic at this point). The most important part of all of this though is that, in spite of how tired I would become by the end of the week, I tried to maintain perfect quality throughout all ten days!

Be careful not to just work, work, work, for the sake of wearing yourself out. You will get tired enough in this period without banging your head against the wall. In the lactic workouts I demand the same quality of paddling I intend to race with. I did the same in the technique and short course workouts. In the long endurance sessions I push myself while staying in the aerobic range and take advantage of the recovery this gives me. When I do the lactic endurance and lactic tolerance, I give it everything while demanding good execution in the moves. I picture how I would like to be paddling in the last four or five gates of the course and force myself to maintain this level of quality.

One thing to keep in mind through all of this is that loading your training for this phase gives you a very limited advantage, if at all. I like it because it gives my final five weeks a controllable shape and an aggressive edge going into the race. However, if I have any sort of physical trouble (injuries or that sort of thing) during this heavy week five I take a break until it goes away. Do not risk a healthy race day for the sake of a small physical and mental advantage.

## Week 4

Week four is really a patchwork week. The first two or three days are appended onto week 5. These are hard and heavy days that finish the overload of your body that you began the week before. By Wednesday you should be completely worn out and ready to take a break, which is exactly what you should spend the remainder of week 4 doing.

I typically spend about three or four days training just enough to keep familiar with the boat and resting the rest of the time. You are not going to get yourself back to full recovery in these three or four days since you are so completely worn down at this point but you should recover to a point where you are now able to train well again. What few workouts you do in this last half of the week should be very technically orientated and should be done at relatively low intensity.

## Week 3

Week three begins an easier training cycle. In week 3 you will do an easier-medium load of training.

I like to actually train at race pace in several workouts this week while keeping the volume of training quite low. For example I might do two separate full-length workouts this week but would only actually do two or three runs per workouts. I might do the same in a lactic-endurance workout by doing 2/3rds of the normal volume while keeping my intensity at a normal level.

One thing you cannot scrimp on at this point is quality. Make every full-length a mock race and make sure that each of your technical and endurance workouts maintains a high degree of quality in their courses and in the way you approach these workouts. From the start of the three week period on you will have a limited amount of time on the water so take as much advantage of that water time as possible.

Look to complete this week feeling quite good—although not being completely recovered. At any point during this week you should feel like you are fresh at the start of your workouts and that your general body fatigue (how tired you are as a whole), is very low. Work to feel energized and excited this whole week.

### Week 2

Week 2 is a important. The objective is to finish this week completely recovered and ready to race a full week in advance!

Typically I would spend the last week at the actual race site itself. I would get water time on the course, there will be people to race, and I usually like to paddle every day just to make sure I am paddling well. You are going to have lots of good reasons why you want to be training during week one. If you start that week in need of a rest and also in need of lots of different practice sessions you might be tempted to train anyway until you are too tired to race effectively.

Instead, take a break so that you are rested on the Sunday before the race. This way you are familiar once again with what complete rest feels like, you will feel good in your workouts throughout the week, and you'll have a little extra juice to spend if you need to train more than you had originally planned.

### Week 1

The key to the last week is keeping your cool and taking care of yourself. You are most likely not going to have good workouts every day. It is also likely that you are going to want to train more than you should. Follow these guidelines when training the last week before a race:

* Instead of working through a problem try and let them go and come back to them if it is something that needs to be fixed before the race. An example might be if you are working on learning how to cross a particular hole on the racecourse. If you beat your head in trying this same move again and again you will find that you are too tired to move by the end of the workout. A better option would be to spend that workout somewhere else and then come back to this move after you've watched others do it successfully.

* Keep your workouts short and focused. I have seen so many people doing run after run down the course the week before the race. Try and limit your runs to two or three per workout.

You want to be FRESH for the race, not worn out from training too much that week. I tend to do no more than one workout per day in the week before the race. You can let your fitness go for a week and still be fine for the rest of the season.

* Don't focus on trying to master every individual move in the course. In famously difficult World Cup sites like Augsburg and Seu there are so many unique moves that can be set. Each of these moves seems to have its own unique recipe for success and I have seen paddlers waste every ounce of energy trying to master each one. Forget about learning everything and focus on getting a feel for the course. Try to figure out how to make the boat move in general. If there is a tricky move set in the end don't worry about it. If you watch a local do it during demonstration runs you'll be as ready as anyone.

* Be sure to do a full-length workout at some point during this last week. You'll want to know what it feels like to race on the course. In evaluating this workout decide if your pacing was appropriate to the course length. Ideally this workout will give you an idea of what to expect in the upcoming race.

I tend to avoid using a standard schedule for any part of this entire five-week plan. Each race has a twist to it that makes it different. By sitting down before each big event and making out a plan that is specific to that situation you can be sure you have an ideal schedule.

With these schedules, as with every training week, be sure to be flexible with your training. Coming into a week with a plan does not mean that you must do this plan to the letter. If training times, injuries, or team dynamics interfere with your planned routine then compromise as much as you need too to optimize your training. Keep in mind the goal of each time period though. If you are supposed to be resting and your training schedule is making you even more tired then you should change your training schedule. The opposite is also true.

Your five weeks should feel like your training is coming at you in smaller and smaller waves. Your fifth week should be very hard, then you should have a very full recovery in the fourth week. Your third week should be decidedly medium followed by a second week that is an easy medium. Finally your last week should be just enough to prepare for the race.

## Race Day

How you race, and what strategies you use to be successful in a race are almost entirely unique to who you are. If you are having trouble with your racing you are not alone. Most paddlers need to learn to race before they can be consistently successful.

My personal experience has been that the more prepared you are for a race run the better you will do. When I was nineteen all but one of the top men's kayaks from Canada and America moved to my training site in Chilliwack, British Columbia. At a time when I had only raced in one international race (at the age of 16) there were four kayaks in my training group who had finished in the top ten in the World. While we didn't all do every workout together, we did get together once a week for Saturday morning full-length race practice.

I am sure that now, years later, every one of those athletes will dispute this claim, but by the second year of training with those athletes I won every single standard full-length workout for the entire winter.

The interesting thing though is that we would occasionally hold "mock-races" -workouts in which we completely imitated a real race. My success in the mock-race workouts was about thirty-percent-much lower than in a normal workout-even though I was paddling at about the same level.

The reason why was that I treated every full-length workout like a true race. I did a double warm-up in the morning. I carefully walked and visualized the course and I raced like I had to win. On an average full-length workout this gave me an advantage over the athletes who just showed up for the workout and climbed on the water.

During the mock races however everyone would do the same preparation I did and the playing field would go level again, for the time being. It did not take me long to realize that the quality of my race preparation would drastically affect the level at which I raced and I set about optimizing my race preparation routine. From that experience this is the race preparation I developed.

### Getting ready to race

At some point you want to get a little more organized about the logistics of your race. Just showing up at the Olympic selection trials and hoping to bum something to eat and a place to sleep on somebody's floor is not a good recipe for success. Take the time a month in advance to call up a good hotel and get reservations. Also make sure you're ready to deal

Photo by Chris Smith.

with everything from broken boats to cold wet rainy days. At the 2000 U.S. Olympic trials I spent the evening before race day number two patching my boat in a hotel room while a brewing rain and slush storm prepared to dump on us the next morning. This was also the day I made the Olympic team!

A key thing to keep in mind about racing is that it is a skill that must be refined the same as any other skill in this sport. You must have a routine that you refine throughout your career and that you simply repeat on race day. The morning of the race is no time to be "winging it" with new ideas or different ways to prepare for the race.

I look at successful racing as going out and preventing as many things from going wrong that I can. I usually go out on demonstration run day (you'll have tons of time on demo-day while they construct the course) and fill the car up with gas, shop for groceries and get situated in my hotel room. This is also a good time to get checked into the race and get your hands on a race schedule.

On a psychological side I find that races tend to wear me out. It is easy to spend every waking hour worrying about the race until you are sick of the whole event and ready to be done with it. I tend to put the race away when I'm not able to constructively work on it and then focus only on the race when I am.

I also tend to not sweat the small stuff. Many of the people at big races are tense and argumentative. It is easier to stay away from all the controversy than to get involved in it. At my first team trials in South Bend, Indiana the organizers set a very difficult move that many of us thought was impossible. U.S. team member Brian Brown was right there with the rest of us while we looked at it and complained amongst ourselves that it needed to be changed. The difference with him, and I remember this as clear as day, was that just after saying he thought it was impossible he shrugged his shoulders and said, "Well, better figure out how to do it." Then he smiled and walked to the other side for a closer look. You can guess who made that team the first day.

The lesson I've learned over the years has been that this is a relative race. You only need to beat your competitors and they will be as challenged as you are with any circumstance. It is best to be completely prepared for the situations you can handle and roll with the punches on the ones you can't. In the long run things will get sorted in the end.

### Demonstration runs

Ignore the course map. They are a waste of time now that you don't get to read them before your last training session. The race really gets going when the course is actually constructed and demonstration runs are getting ready to start.

I like to arrive about thirty minutes before demonstration runs. This is about as late as I can get there and still have time to make a preliminary race plan before the demos start. If you take longer to make a race plan, try and arrive a little earlier.

This preliminary race plan is important because you

need to identify what sort of questions you want the forerunners to answer for you on this first run through the course. I make a line and then use the forerunners to decide if my line is possible, if there is a better line that I haven't thought of and how difficult my line is to execute. It is also important to see how the water pushes the boat throughout the course. Especially in wide rivers you may not get another chance untill the race to see exactly what the current is doing in the gates themselves. If the forerunners are good enough you can often find out exactly how tight you will be able to cut a certain move and still get away with it.

Be wary of this though, often the demonstration runners aren't racing because they didn't qualify for this race. Your skills probably far out shine their own.

It is hard to beat a watch for evaluating which way to do a certain move. As a matter of course I almost always split all the paddlers on the trickier moves or if a move can be done in more than one way. The watch will often give you enough information to decide for yourself how to do a certain move. Be wary of always trying to do each move the quickest way though. Often you must weigh the risks of gaining tenths of a second against making a major race-ending error.

## Making a race plan

I always start making a race plan immediately after the last forerunner has finished their run. By this point you should already have had a plan, modified that plan, and have a new rough idea of what you want to do.. This time through the course you are going to polish that plan into a strategy that will win this race. I do this by starting at the finish and working up from the bottom.

You are going to make a race plan that is faster than your competitors and easier to execute. Think of it this way: if you watch the best billiard players in the world they will rarely make a difficult shot, instead they will continue to sink easy shot after easy shot. The reason why is that each time they hit the ball they are aiming to not only sink their target ball, but also set themselves up for their next shot. Thus each hit they leave the ball exactly where they need to for the easiest possible shot on their next strike. I make a race plan the same way-by starting from the finish line and working backwards.

When I was beginning to race people often told me to always be thinking about the next gate, always be thinking a gate ahead the entire way down the course. That is crazy! You have enough to think about just concentrating on what you are doing. Put together a race strategy now that already takes that next gate, and every gate after it, into consideration. Now is the time to think, later there will only be time for racing.

I will begin making a race plan by looking at the last gate to the finish line. Once I have found the best line between the two I look at gates 24 to 25 (let's assume it is a 25 gate course). When I make a strategy from gate 24 I choose a line that goes on the best line from gate 24 to where I need to be to

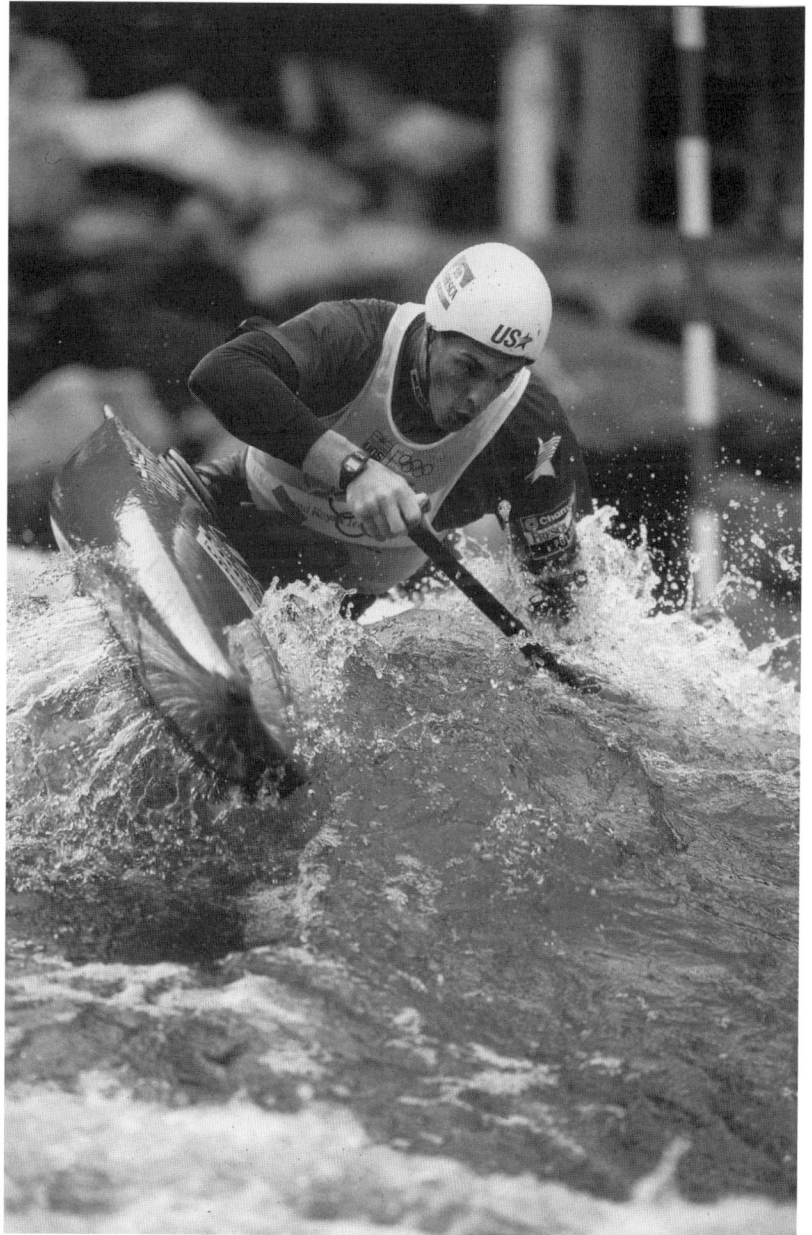

Photo by Chris Smith.

execute the best line from gate 25 to the finish!

The best example of this was on a race I did on the Ocoee once. The last gate was a downstream just in the eddy on the way to the finish. It was quite easy to aim directly at gate 25 from gate 24 and sprint for the finish line. This line took the paddler directly through gate 25 and then down a slow shallow eddy to the finish line. In this race I gained a second or more on every single paddler by doing a wider cross that gave me room to cut from gate 25 back into the current and down a faster line to the finish.

An average paddler makes a race plan from the top down. For each gate they choose the fastest line to the next gate and will beat you gate to gate on many of the easier gates. But they'll blow out and lose time in the more difficult moves. An elite paddler will make a plan from the bottom up so that as they paddle down the course they link turn after turn. Each hard move is executed quickly and sharply because the move is easy when you approach it this way.

Here are some tips to putting together a fast race plan:

* Almost every race that is worth anything will have its hard move. It's not any particular part of this move that makes it hard, but rather the sum of them. For example: a course designer has set a downstream gate in an eddy just below a ledge. You must jump the ledge, land on the eddy line and guide your boat into the eddy, through the gate, and back out of the eddy so you can quickly head downstream. If you were to charge straight down on this move you would have to:
* jump the ledge.
* deal with the eddyline.
* turn into the eddy far enough to make the gate.
* avoid the poles as you wiggle into the gate.
* turn back out of the eddy and into the current.
On the other hand, if you were to approach from the side you would already be heading into the eddy, this would allow you to skip over the eddyline without having to use it to turn into the eddy. If you also were to aim a little above the gate early in your approach you could be turning downstream as you jump.

Think about what you've done in relation to what we worked on in flatwater gates: this approach has given the boat its ideal placement, near the eddyline, its ideal trajectory, at the gate, and its ideal spin-momentum, downstream through the gate and back out into the current. This paddler will only need to do a jump stroke back into a rudder to cruise through the gate and back out into the current.

How did the second paddler make a hard move easy? The first paddler had a lot of trouble with this move because he had to do so many things at one time. This second paddler spread out the hard move so that he had time to do each element of the move separately. By the time he arrived at the gate he simply had to jump and ride the move out.

* Try and spend as little time in eddies as possible. This means that you will want to set up your approaches to upstreams such that you need only cross the eddyline, do a short quick turn and get back into the current. For downstreams in eddies you will generally want to nip into the eddy, through the gate and back into the current. If you must cross an eddy or paddle down through an eddy then etch into your mind that you will sprint those few strokes to quickly get back into the current.
* Decide in advance where you want to go hard and where you will want to go slow. There will be places in your race run where you will wish you had the energy to give a full burst of speed. Decide in advance where these places are and be sure you don't burn yourself out before you reach them. There are also some moves, like some difficult offsets in fast current, where you will be faster if you slow the boat down before you get there.
* After training on the course for several days you will have many pre-conceived notions about how to do certain moves. In many cases this will help. But be careful to have an open mind. There have been plenty of times when I tried to do a move a certain way that felt great in training while my competitors did a more obvious and simple line that took seconds off my time.

Once I have designed a race plan I almost immediately go from the top down with a coach. I find that saying the course out loud to someone is often the best way to ensure you have a complete race plan. If you have trouble describing your race plan to your coach then it is most likely not clear in your head.

My coach, Sylvan Poberaj, is an especially good sounding board for this in that he rarely interrupts this process. Most often he will let me describe an entire section before offering up a differing opinion if he has one. He is also fantastic in that he doesn't have to have a differing opinion. If he likes my strategy he doesn't interrupt my chain of thought. In fact we will typically continue to walk the entire time I am describing the course so that I come as close as possible to offering up an uninterrupted monologue on the course as possible.

Only after I have finished this final walk down the course do I go home for dinner. This way I can put the race away when I'm not completely concentrating on it so I do not stop to worry about the race again until I'm ready for bed.

I visualize best when I am relaxed and in a quiet place. Before I go to bed I usually go out for a walk or a sit on the porch and go through the course in my head. I will visualize the course several more times before I begin my race run and this first one is really a rudimentary version of the final vision. Early on my visualizations are a composite of what I've seen from each shore of the river with what I remember from training on that whitewater. By the time I do my final visualization of the course I will see the course the way I would see it in the race. Believe it or not this often, for some reason, includes my hands pumping away in my peripheral vision, which is something I never notice while paddling.

Once I am in bed I will visualize the course again. This often feels like work and will put me to sleep just after I finish my run. I follow this up with a visualization of my entire run the moment I wake up in the morning. This is often my best visualization because I wake up with nothing else on my mind and can run through the entire course without having my mind wander onto different subjects.

## Race Preparation

Everything I do is set out on a schedule that I've made the night before. This way I'll know as soon as I finish breakfast, or my walk, or stretching, if I'm ahead or behind schedule. This gives me the chance to catch up if I'm late. It also allows the security to not leave too early if I'm ahead.

I am finicky about what I eat on race day. I like to race a little bit hungry. I hate racing on a full stomach so I follow a pretty strict diet on race day. My favorite race day meal is four pieces of plain wheat bread, two pieces of fruit, and a lot of water. When I race out of the country I often can't find wheat bread and substitute power bars instead. While this sounds like a bland way to start your day I find that it sits well in my stomach while I warm up and race and it lasts quite a while. I'll also bring a little extra food with me to the course to eat directly after first runs.

After eating I'll go out right away for a quick walk/jog. I basically walk because it makes my stretching easier and more effective. You have probably already noticed that you'll need a lot of flexibility to paddle the way I do. A good stretch goes a long way towards getting me ready to race.

I have a set stretching routine that I actually do every day before I train. It takes me about thirty minutes every morning and I do it in its entirety on race day. I stretch my entire upper body, emphasizing rotation and hip flexibility since these are the elements most important to good performance in a race. Directly after stretching I drive to the course for my early warm-up.

I first began doing a double warm-up after visiting the Olympic training center in Colorado Springs. They had mentioned that we should all be warming up better and warming down better at our races. Warming up twice was one of their suggestions that I found worked well for me in training.

The first time I did this at an international race I found that I felt much better in the starting gate and all of the top ten or twenty boats in the world were there! Almost everyone but us Americans were getting out and doing an early paddle before the race.

The sports-science people also said that we should be warming down for at least fifteen minutes at a medium pace after every run. Again you'll find that top boats internationally will do the same thing-taking the time to clean the lactic acid out of their blood after every run.

My first warm up largely ignores whatever gates are set up for practicing. I like to put in and slowly paddle for five or ten minutes gradually increasing my pace as I go. While I do this I visualize my run again, often closing my eyes as I paddle to fully see the course in my head. Once I have run through the course and feel warmed up enough I pause to stretch and spin the boat a bit to warm up my turning muscles. Sometimes taking the time to sit there allows my warm-up to sink in a little better.

When I'm ready, I point my boat back towards the put in and do a full length run on the flatwater. This is done at race pace and includes every turn, pivot, lean and stroke that I will do on my actual race run. It is a great way to kinetically feel your way through a visualization. I often feel like this is the most important visualization of my entire day. In many ways this completes the entire picture of what my run is going to be like. I'll make this a part of my race routine regardless of how little flatwater is available for my warm-up.

I always schedule at least an hour between when I've finished warming up and changed into dry clothes and when I must get back into my wet

clothes for my first run. I take this hour to walk the course again, watch competitors do their runs, and speak with coaches about how to do certain moves. It is important to remain flexible about your race plan throughout the entire race. As more and more people come down the course you will get a much clearer picture about how to do the course. Be ready to roll with these changes. At World Cup races I often have twenty minutes or less between when the first kayak goes down the course and when I must start. I won the World Cup in 1997 based on information my coach gave me over the radio forty-five seconds before I entered the starting gate!

How early I get on the water for my final warm-up depends largely on the situation, but I look to get changed at thirty minutes before my run and be on the water twenty minutes before my run. Time always seems to disappear on me and I usually feel like I get just enough of a warm-up in before my run starts. On this warm-up I also start out slower but work into my turning moves much quicker. I also add in some sprints and at least two pieces that last a minute or so and are just below race pace. I try and keep the boat moving between the harder efforts so that I continue to warm-up for the entire twenty minutes and also to prevent any build up of lactic acid.

Early on in this warm-up I will visualize the course again while I paddle. As I get down to the last five minutes I will do one last quick visualization of the course as I begin to feel the pressure mount. This last visualization is usually done at a standstill as I rest up for my run.

I usually enter the starting gate soon after the last paddler has left or when I have a minute left if there is a larger interval between paddlers. Once in the gate I focus only on what I have to do in the first few gates. I run through start to gate one or two over and over in my head. Nothing else comes in, just start to gate one. Then when the little box quits beeping I go like hell.

Photo by Chris Smith.

# The Workouts

## Introduction

This last section is simply a list of common workouts for whitewater slalom. Included in this list are many of the workouts we do for all types of endurance, lactic, and strength/technique training. This is by no means a complete list, but it is a starting point for you to begin your training. You will constantly be adding to and adapting from this list to make your training interesting and directly focused on your priorities.

There are several conventions I use in this section that should be explained:

All these workouts, though described in text, are listed with mathematical notation. For example if you are going to do two sets of five runs through a loop that is two minutes long, and then you rest thirty seconds between each start in a set, I would note that as 2 x 5(2'on, 30" off). In a gym it would be expressed as two sets of five times two minutes on with thirty seconds rest. In standard notation it is expressed as:

**[(# of sets) x  (# of repetitions)(Time on, Time resting)]**

Every workout also has a recommended intensity. Rather than describing each pace separately I have used the standard U.S. team descriptions.

There are three endurance paces:

**End. 1:** This is your easiest endurance pace. Many people also call this pace "recovery endurance." You should be paddling comfortably, though with good posture and technique. This pace should just allow you to carry on a conversation throughout your workout. For the average person this rate corresponds to a pulse between 140-155.

**End. 2:** This is the workhorse pace of your aerobic work. It is really the hardest pace you can maintain for forty minutes or more. This should be hard enough that any sustained conversation leaves you breathless. For the average person this pace corresponds to a pulse between 155-170

**End. 3:** This pace should leave you on fire when you are done. This is the pace you should use for most of your lactic-endurance pieces. For me this is simply the hardest pace I can sustain without fading over the given period of time. If I was going to do a three minute piece I would go as hard as I could and still maintain that pace over three minutes. For the average person this pace corresponds to a pulse above 165+ and the intensity would depend on the duration of on time.

**Race Pace:** You should spend your  year becoming familiar with this pace. This is the pace that corresponds to your ultimate run on a slalom course. This pace is used in virtually all kinds of workouts that are meant to mimic a race run.

**60's pace:** This is the pace you would typically use on a half-length run. It is faster than your race pace but is still paced enough that you can maintain good technique and lines over the length of the course.

**Full-Speed:** This is a completely un-paced effort. You must leave the starting gate at your most viscously fast pace and your rate should fade from there. Make this a full sprint from the very beginning.

The workouts are divided into four sections, as described in my section on yearly training. They are strength/shorts, lactic, lactic-endurance, and long endurance. Rotate through these workouts based on priority and time of year. Good luck with your training.

## Workout: 2 x 8(45"on, 2'15 med.)

Type: Lactic Endurance

Protocol: This is an active rest workout. The idea is that for each of your 24 min. sets you never stop paddling. Set a course comparable to a race course that is about 45 seconds long. Now do that course at race pace; no need to go faster. When you are finished with the course continue to paddle at a medium pace for two minutes and fifteen seconds. For those of you keeping track that is a total of three minutes. I usually finish the course, back off the pace, and continue to paddle downstream for twenty seconds or more. From this point you can head back to the start and arrive at just the right time.

People always get confused about how this works until they do it so there are a couple of things to keep in mind. First off, you only start every three minutes so if you get back to the start early do circles or something until it is time to go. Secondly, since you start every three minutes, and so do your training partners, you should never catch up to them. I don't know how many times I've been training with somebody who was so excited to be catching my training partners and me at loops, only to find out he was tangling up the whole workout!

Intensity: Race pace for the forty-five second part, much mellower for the medium part. Usually in the fall and winter my medium is End 2. In the spring, while I'm more interested in executing the course well, my medium is End 1.

This is a fantastic endurance workout to focus on race technique. I essentially think of it as 16 x 45-second race runs. Since there is plenty of time to make it back to the start you can train on pretty decent whitewater and make a very good effort at each run. In the fall and winter this workout is more of a Fartlek, or active recovery, long endurance session. In the spring it is truly lactic loops and each run is prepared for and executed as if it were a race run.

Personal Notes:

## Workout: Shadow Loops: 2 x 8(45" on, 2'15 med.)

Type: Lactic-Endurance

Protocol: These are similar to the 45"on, 2'15 medium except they are done on flatwater and they are done when you don't have access to gates! Simply keep the boat moving across the lake. At every three minutes start a forty-five second Imaginary Piece! Typically I do my pieces while visualizing sections from the previous year's world cup, working my way sequentially through each course throughout the workout. That's all there is to it. Simply close your eyes and paddle the way you would if you were on whitewater. When you get to gate three, an upstream, do an upstream right there in the flat and keep going.

Intensity: You should be going race pace for the on time, the forty-five seconds, and End 2 for the medium paced stuff.

This is a fantastic way to get in a complete slalom orientated flatwater workout without having to find a training course. I use this workout a lot when I go up to work at the Dagger plant and only have access to a lake for workouts. It is also one of the best ways I know to work your visualization skills. I did a similar workout, but doing entire race runs together, in 1991. I finished each run within four seconds of what my race time had been at that race, that year.

Personal Notes:

## Workout: McLoops: 45" course x (1,2,4,2,1,2,4,2,1 runs)

Type: Lactic Endurance

Protocol: This workout is a fantastic way to train your lactic endurance and is a mainstay of many training programs. Set a 45 second gate loop on a course similar to a race course (you can really do this anywhere). Do a single run, and then rest for a single run. Then you do two runs, and rest for two runs. Do the same thing for four runs, two runs, one run, two runs, four runs, two runs and then one run. The workout originally got its name, "M-loops" from the shape of these "repetition pyramids." Larry Norman, a Canadian C-1, began to call it "McLoops" from the way "M-loops" looked in his training log.

Another variation of this workout is to do it with a training partner. This workout can be done completely without a watch. Simply do a run, then have your partner do a run. By doing each set sequentially your partner should give you equal rest since you must wait while they are going (Note: it actually sucks to be the second person in this, so always volunteer to go first).

Intensity: Your intensity should be very hard. This is a workout where you truly want to go lactic. Don't let yourself use your four run pace for your shorter pieces, instead go as hard as you can for each distance.

This workout is very close to being what I would call lactic tolerance. It is a great workout to begin lactic training in early spring before you truly begin to do full out lactic tolerance.

Personal Notes:

## Workout: 2 x 10(2'on, 30" off)

Type: Lactic Endurance

Protocol: Do a two minute piece followed by a short thirty seconds of rest. These should be done in sets of ten, which makes for a long workout. Set the course in a loop. Usually this loop would be made to be two minutes long, but I like to set it so that I go two minutes and come up a little short of the start gate again. This way I can cruise along easily for thirty seconds and not have to sit still while I wait for your next start..

Intensity: Essentially you are going for two minutes at End 2 pace, and then resting just long enough to freshen up for your next run. This is a long workout, but each run is short enough that you are tempted to go pretty hard early on. Its alright to be drawn into this since you want this to be lactic endurance, but do the workout once before you go absolutely nuts. I think you'll find it's a long ways to go after the first few if you go too hard.

This is a great way to get both long and lactic endurance. I tend to use this workout after the fall when I'm getting ready to start putting some intensity into my endurance workouts. The total workout time is forty minutes, but since you get a little break between each run it can be more intense than just a straight forty minute set.

Personal Notes:

## Workout:  2 x 6(2' on, 1' off)

Type:  Lactic Endurance

Protocol:  Two minute loops with an emphasis on race practice.  Rest should be complete, but keep moving the entire time. The course should have a hard move in it, and the entire course, at least on the way down, should be set at the same difficulty as the race you are preparing for.

Intensity:  Go at race pace for these.  You should strive to maintain both this pace, and the quality that you'd like to see on a race run.

This is a fantastic workout during the racing season. If you think about it, you'll get twelve runs at race pace on a racecourse.  That is a fantastic amount of quality practice for one session. You should emphasize quality and cleanliness.  Compared to the workouts you've been doing, this is not a lot of volume and your pain level should be relatively tolerable so be perfect!

Personal Notes:

## Workout: 2 x 4(3' on, 30"off)

Type:  Lactic Endurance

Protocol:  Set the course as a loop.  Go for three minutes, resting for thirty seconds between runs.  Do four of these per set and give yourself about five to seven minutes between sets so that each set has a lot of quality.

Intensity:  This is an intense workout.  Go at End 3 and emphasize keeping your pace up throughout the set.  Remember that you only need to last thirteen and a half minutes before you get a break.

These are very intense loops.  They make a great way to add a little variation to the three-minute loops with longer rest.  It is also a short enough set that you can both go hard and feel like you're getting away with something by leaving the workout sooner than most.  I don't recommend that you, in an attempt to make this one harder, do more runs per set.  Three-minute loops are intense by nature.  If you want to do more then give yourself a minute rest between sets so that each effort has more quality.

Personal Notes:

### Workout: 10(3'on, 1'off)

Type:  Lactic-Endurance

Protocol:  Do three minutes at End 3 followed by one minute of semi-active rest.  Usually athletes set the course in a loop.  This way you can start and stop at the same place.  If I am in a hurry I'll do all ten of these in a row.  That way it takes me forty-minutes, start to finish.  Normally though this is meant to be a pretty intense Lactic-Endurance workout so it works well to do two sets of five.  This way I can take a rest in the middle and keep my intensity at full blast throughout the workout.

INTENSITY: These should be very hard loops.  There are many different kinds of 3 minute loops, some with shorter rest and some with longer.  The longer you rest, the faster you can go, and the more lactic acid you will build up.  While you must pace this workout somewhat to make it through all thirty minutes, you still need to push the limit of your ability.  Go as hard as you can go, and let the upper limit of your pain threshold limit your pace.

Personal Notes:

### Workout: 8(3'on, 2'off)

Type:  Lactic-Endurance

Protocol:  Set the course about as hard as the race you are training for.  I usually have a pretty standard gate combination with one move that is quite difficult, just to spice things up.  Do your three minute piece hard, but then keep moving a bit between runs.  You should be feeling it after each run, so take some of your rest time to paddle it off, and spend some time evaluating your run.

Intensity:  These should be done at race pace, End 3.  Each run is essentially a long race run all bundled into one.  The long rest should allow you to recover sufficiently to the point where you can really open up on your next run.  These are about as close to being full lactic pieces as you can get without going over the edge.

   This is a fantastic workout for hustle.  There will be several times that you are so tired that your boat loses speed, or you lose the thread on the course.  Use that time to pick it up and get the boat moving again.  For the most part you are dealing with a lot of race fatigue.  You shouldn't be as bad off as during a lactic tolerance workout, but you should feel about as tired as you would towards the bottom of a race run.  Become very familiar with this feeling and learn to perform within its grasp.  You can easily win a race by simply being the best one there at dealing with the pain at the bottom of your run.

Personal Notes:

## Workout: 6(3' on, 6' med)

Type: Lactic Endurance

Protocol: Paddle across a lake at a medium pace to warm up. Then, do three-minute pieces at race pace followed by six minutes of easy paddling.

Intensity: Go at End 3 for the on time, for the medium time you should maintain End 2. The idea is that you go over your lactic threshold, but then recover actively from that state. What this means is that you will be burning like a race run after your on time, but rather than taking some time off to recover quickly from this effort you will keep some pressure on and slowly recover over about four minutes.

These workouts are called "Fartlek Endurance" after an unfortunately named physiologist who invented them. They are a great way to raise your threshold level but have another advantage for slalom athletes. I use this workout to get a real firm grip on what my race pace will be. There are several places on a race course where you will need to juice your boat along to make a certain move, or to speed up after losing some momentum. There will be many more places where you will need to back off and pace yourself at a rate you can sustain for 120 seconds. This is a great workout to familiarize yourself with that pace.

Personal Notes:

## Workout: 6(5' on, 1' off)

Type: Lactic-Endurance

Protocol: Five minute loops done typically on easier water with a fairly simple course. For most training courses this will mean that you need to do two or more loops through your course. Your rest should be somewhat active, at least enough to shake off your run.

Intensity: This can be either End 2 or a fairly easy End 3. These loops are typically done as a medium level workout. For the most part I try and not get overly lactic in these loops. Instead I use a pace that would be similar to doing a hard jog.

This workout is essentially another way to do quality medium length endurance. Try and focus on having good, consistent execution of my upstreams and to glide through all of the moves as much as possible. Often my main objective for this workout is to keep the boat moving and to do all the upstreams in two strokes.

Personal Notes:

## Workout: "Brute Loops", 2 x 20 min. Power Endurance

Type: Lactic-Endurance

Protocol: Set a course that is the same difficulty you will be racing on. Then, for two twenty minute pieces, paddle up at a medium pace, and back down through the gates at race pace.

Intensity: Race pace in the gates, and End 2 for the paddle back to the top.

This is the hardest of the hard workouts. There are lots of things that make it worse than it actually has to be. You should become much to tired to reliably make all the gates well, you may get too tired to make all of the attainments back up to the top, and you may find it hurts so much you want to stop. Resist the urge to make it easy on yourself! This workout is supposed to hurt badly. It is a test of your will, stop whining and paddle! Someday I'm going to name a breakfast cereal after this workout.

Personal Notes:

## Workout: Phase Change Loops 5(5' on, 2' off)

Type: Lactic-Endurance

Protocol: Set a course that has several cases in it where you would, in a race situation, pick up your pace to avoid losing time. Some examples are downstreams in eddys, an upstream where you must exit by crossing quick current to another upstream or a downstream on the same wire, or a downstream to downstream combination where you must cross an eddy in the middle. Put these into a normal course and do the course at a normal pace, End 2. When you get to the parts where you need to put on some power to avoid losing boat speed, hit the gas like crazy! I mean go, go, go at a full sprint! You are trying to accentuate the difference between your normal pace and the pace you use in these important sections. After you pass the critical spot let your boat glide back down to normal (End 2 pace).

Intensity: End 2 for most of your runs; full sprint in the moves.

This is a hybrid workout. You are training yourself to come out of your normal pace and goose the boat where that would prove to be a big advantage. In the overall strategy of a run there are places where you can save a full second or two by sprinting at full pace. There are many more places where sprinting does nothing more than wear you out, only putting you a percent or so ahead of your competitors in that section. Use this workout to learn to conserve you energy until, by pouncing on a move, you can truly leap ahead of your worn out competitors.

Another good lesson to learn from this workout was that it was born of the necessity to train my body to react instinctively to these sorts of opportunities. I constantly adapt physical workouts, like five-minute loops in this case, to achieve technical goals. Learn to this yourself with your workouts.

Personal Notes:

## Workout:  Pursuit Loops 3(15' on, 3' off)

Type:  Lactic-Endurance

Protocol:  Do three sets of fifteen-minute pieces on a looped gate course with a training partner of similar ability.  Take turns starting thirty seconds behind each other.  Once started go at a mind-bending pace until you catch, or avoid catching your training partner.  Once caught remain at an End 2-3 level and continue on with a team run loop until that piece ends.

Intensity:  Go at End 3 for the pursuit part of the loop. If you do catch your training partner you will most likely slow a little to a more reasonable pace so that they won't run you down on the next piece.

Comments:  You need a truly keen training partner for this workout.  I have nearly killed myself doing them with former teammates and training partners of mine Rich Weiss and Eric Jackson.  However, I've found everyone else completely uninterested in chasing, or being chased, for that amount of time. Kids these days...

Personal Notes:

## Workout:  3(10' on, 2' off)

Type:  Long Endurance

Protocol:  Ten minute pieces done on easy water.  The paddle back to the start should not involve any noticeable increase in pace.  You should have a constant pace throughout your run.  Rest can be total, or with a little moving around to shake off your effort

Intensity:  Your pace should be a consistent End 2. This workout should not, ideally, involve anything that requires an increase in pace over more than just a few strokes.  Try and maintain a steady rate, usually beyond the comfort zone, but without going lactic.

   This workout can be used as either long endurance or, when done at an easier pace, a recovery workout. Typically I would do this workout in the fall as a shorter length hard endurance workout.  This workout was done right at my threshold and was the shorter counter part of 3 x 15 min. loops.
   In the spring I would do this as a recovery workout and would reign the pace in considerably.  Typically I would try and stay within a zone where I felt comfortable while I paddled.  This usually meant that I started off slowly and increased my pace as I worked my way into the workout.

Personal Notes:

## Workout: 3(15' on, 2' off)

Type: Long Endurance

Protocol: Fifteen minute pieces done on easy water. The paddle back to the start should not involve any noticeable increase in pace. You should have a constant pace throughout your run. Rest can be total, or with a little moving around to shake off your effort

Intensity: Your pace should be a consistent End 2. This workout should not, ideally, involve anything that requires an increase in pace over more than just a few strokes. Try and maintain a steady rate, usually beyond the comfort zone, but without going lactic.

This workout can be a great way to work your aerobic system. In the fall, winter, and early spring I work in periods a lot. Usually in a hard week I'll do three or four times a fifteen minute piece. It is a long enough piece that you are working primarily your aerobic system, but with the breaks every fifteen minutes you can still keep a pretty good pace and maintain quality. I use this as a fairly hard workout and tend to do ten minute pieces if I'm going to go a little easier. For this workout I focus on working well while tired, and being as efficient as possible. You should try and nail every move that you do, without paddling at race pace for more than a few strokes at a time (just enough to nail the move, then back it off to aerobic pace again).

Personal Notes:

## Workout: 2(20'on, 2' off)

Type: Long Endurance

Protocol: Two sets of twenty-minute pieces across a lake, typically done without gates.

Intensity: This workout can be done at almost any speed. End 1 for recovery, Aer 2 to work strictly aerobic, and End 3 if you'd like to burn it up across the lake.

Two times twenty minutes across a lake is the most standard workout in the book. I use this in the fall and winter as my longer endurance in a slalom boat (any longer and I tend to use a wildwater boat so my legs don't fall asleep). For these workouts I tend to go pretty hard. In the spring it is a great recovery from some of the lactic stuff or a great way to do medium level endurance without wearing out all your slalom muscles. Whichever way you do this use it as a time to focus on proper posture, proper stroke technique, and to limit the amount that your boat rocks from side to side. I find it necessary, at whichever pace I choose, to spend a few seconds out of every five minutes or so evaluating and improving some aspect of my stroke. See the section on stroke drills to find some good exercises for improving your stroke technique.

Personal Notes:

## Workout: 30 minute "paddle about"

Type:  Long Endurance

Protocol:  Spend thirty or more minutes paddling through gates on easy moving or flat water.

Intensity:  Very low, this workout should feel like all you did was warm up for a half hour.

I worked with a British coach who loved to do lactic work, and loved to do this workout.  This workout is a great recovery from the lactic stuff and a great way to focus only on precision and gate execution.  Typically I don't even set a course for this workout.  Instead I make courses as I go, usually working on whatever I feel needs the most help at the time.  This is a great way to work out problems in your technique without the pressure of a coach watching, or a watch timing.

Personal Notes:

## Workout:  40', 60', 90' on

Type:  Long Endurance

Protocol:  Paddle across a lake for a long time.

Intensity:  This workout is usually done at End 2.  The only real exception is the 90'minute pieces, which need to be done at a hard End 1, or an easy End 2.

hese are the workhorses of your fall training.  Some European teams will do these pieces from five to seven times a week!  I don't recommend you waste your valuable time doing that (unless your priorities are fitness or being the marathon champion), but you should get out at least twice a week for these longer workouts.  I tend to do two of these a week mixed in with some longer gate loops and maybe a single, longer, lactic endurance workout just to keep things interesting.

Personal Notes:

## Workout: 60's, 9 x 60"

Type: Peak Lactic

Protocol: Set a slalom course, of similar difficulty to a racecourse, on the best whitewater you have. The course should be between 55 and 70 and have at least one difficult move that you must negotiate on the fly (not right at the start). Do between three to five runs per course before changing the gates and doing another course.

Intensity: You should be pushing yourself above race pace, but still at a rate which you can control and maintain good technique.

This is a great workout to go really fast on whitewater. I find it is a great technical workout also since you have usually not really had time to become extremely tired by the time you finish. Focus on maintaining consistently fast times. You should use this workout to learn how to go fast the FIRST time you leave the starting gate and maintain that speed throughout the workout regardless of other factors. I usually rate my performance in this workout based on, whether I won or not, how many good runs I had, how many clean runs I had, and how smooth I managed to be in the face of an all out effort.

Personal Notes:

## Workout: 60's, 3 x 3(60")

Type: Peak Lactic

Protocol: Set a slalom course, of similar difficulty to a racecourse, on the best whitewater you have. The course should be between 55 and 70 and have at least one difficult move that you must negotiate on the fly (not right at the start). Do two or three runs on this course. Originally we did this workout when we were allowed a practice run and two race runs so we did the workout in this format. I guess now you could just two runs per course. Anyway, change the course every two or three runs. Race like it was the World Championships for every run. The idea is that you get three or four races per workout. Your two runs combined must beat all the competition.

Intensity: You should be pushing yourself above race pace, but still at a rate which you can control and maintain good technique.

This workout is one of the best tools you can use to train yourself to DEMAND performance. Set your sights high. I use this workout to get in the habit of making myself have good runs whenever I need to. Changing the course so often is also a good way to get lots of visualization and race preparation experience all in a single workout. Keep this in mind. There are lots of folks who can be world medallists at sixties, there just isn't that much time to differentiate between paddlers. The winner of a sixties workout is the one who demands flawless runs.

Personal Notes:

## Workout: Offset sixties, 8 x 60"

Type: Peak Lactic

Protocol: Set a slalom course that is entirely offsets. I think it can be good to put some harder moves in this workout, but nothing so ridiculous that the boat has to slow or stop. What you are really trying to set is a course where the boat is moving pretty quickly all the time. The idea is that you are racing down a course that you would normally scramble to make, but you learn to make it smoothly and with less strokes.

Set the course and do your runs slowly at first. Use conservative lines and few strokes on your first few runs. You are trying to get out of the habit of desperately scrambling down the hill, so prepare enough that you are not barely making things. Speed up for the first few runs to a crisp, yet still more relaxed pace. At this point you should be on a line that you can Paddle, which is to say you are not head ducking, bobbing and weaving to make things happen. You should be able to paddle through each of the gates.

For your final few runs really hit the gas. I mean motor! For the first couple of these quick runs (these are really fun), use the same lines you previously worked. After that, make it a free for all, cut the corners where you want. In the end, analyze where you were faster or slower. Try to find where it is faster to head duck or sneak, and where it is faster to sit up and paddle.

Intensity: You should be pushing yourself above race pace, but still at a rate which you can control and maintain good technique.

This is a great workout for offset technique. I think this is much better than doing two or three offsets in a short course workout. Keep in mind the purpose of changing paces throughout the workout so that this doesn't fade into a workout where you are brainlessly pounding out runs. This makes a great workout any time, but I especially like it before a race because it is good practice when you are both trying to recover (it makes a great recovery workout), and wanting to get accustomed to going really really fast (which is what I love about this).

Personal Notes:

## Workout: Fulls, 6 x Race Runs

Type: Peak Lactic

Protocol: This is the most standard of all race workouts. Simply set a racecourse on your best whitewater course. Do five runs on the course timed and scored. You should rest between runs for at least five times the amount of time you spent racing.

Intensity: Do these at race pace, but, depending on the time of year, you can experiment with what your race pace is

This is the bread and butter of full lengths workouts. Most of your race practice during a year will be done in this format. This format is, however, very forgiving and can make the workout less significant than it is. Athletes tend to spend the whole five runs trying to get the same course right. If you are losing after two runs you can still come back and win the workout later. You also can visualize the course quite well for your first few runs before banging out your last few. I set several objectives in this workout to force myself to stay keen throughout my runs. I try to have the single fastest run, to win the first two runs combined, to beat my competition on all five runs, and to have a clean workout. This is a lot to chew in a single workout, but be sure to set your own objectives so that you aren't merely banging out five runs to get the workout done.

Personal Notes:

### Workout:  Mock Race, 2 x full lengths

Type:  Peak Lactic

Protocol:  This workout should be no different than the most intense race you do all season.  If you can, set the course and prepare for the race the night before, just as you'd do in a race.  For races I usually do a double warm-up, so I do the same thing for this workout, paddling about two hours before I start for the race.  Also be sure to make your entire day leading up to the race the same as game day.  I like to set start times in advance with at least an hour between runs to more closely mimic a true race.

Intensity:  Do these at race pace, period.  Be sure to rest at least an hour between runs.

An important part of this workout is the de-briefing after you have finished.  I like to sit down with a piece of paper (my training log), and go through all the mistakes I made throughout the workout.  Was I hungry but forgot food?  Did I feel warmed-up enough at the start?  Was I late for my start?  This workout should get you ready to race and perform at a high level when it really counts. It should also be a dry run of an important race day where you can sort out the particulars of being ready.

Personal Notes:

### Workout:  Fulls, Qualifier/Finals

Type:  Peak Lactic

Protocol: Do a race on Saturday with a typical slalom course.  Do only the two runs of a normal race.  Change the course by only moving six different gates and have another race on Sunday.  If you have a large training group you can stipulate that only so many people go through to the "final" on the second day just to add pressure. In every way the format of both days should match a real race.  See mock race for more information.

Intensity:  Do these at race pace.  Have at least an hour of rest between runs.

One of the hardest parts of both team trials and World Cup races is the fact that, after putting in everything you've got into one day, you must get up the next morning and do it again.  This workout is meant to mimic this amount of pressure and this amount of work.  Typically this will wear you out before the end of the weekend despite being only four runs.  To really make this workout effective you must practice every aspect of your race day.  This includes race warm-ups, visualizing the course, and time in between runs.

Personal Notes:

## Workout:  Course Change fulls, full lengths x 5

Type:  Peak Lactic

Protocol:  Do a standard full-length workout.  The only difference is that after each full-length run you should change one gate on the course.  If you are doing these in a group make sure you stay together to avoid tangling people up with unexpected course changes.

Intensity:  Do these at race pace, but, depending on the time of year, you can experiment with what your race pace is

With the Qualifier/Finals format set up the way they are, the judges are only allowed to make six changes to the course between the Qualifier and the Finals.  This means that, in the final, there will be several times that you charge out of a course that is familiar to you, and into a course that is unfamiliar (you are just as likely to do the opposite).  The idea of this workout is to familiarize you with these types of changes and mentally prepare you for going from the familiar to the unfamiliar and back again.  This workout will also teach you how and when to change your lines so that they mesh with the new moves.  There will be times where what was fast the previous day will make no sense on the new course.

Personal Notes:

## Workout:  (1/3, 2/3, fulls)

Type:  Peak Lactic

Protocol:  Set a full-length course and divide it into three parts.  Do the course in thirds on your first run keeping track of your times throughout.  Keep in mind that you must do this entire workout at race-pace, not faster or slower.  Now do the same course but do the first two thirds before stopping.  Have your coach take a time for each third and also for your final third, which you will do separately.  Finally, do a full-length but have your coach time each third the entire way down.  Compare each of your splits to those on your race run.  Did you notice that your times were too fast on top on your full-length run and that they faded a lot on the bottom?  If they did do the entire workout again, trying to exactly match your best average run down the course, not too fast on top and not to slow at the bottom.

Intensity:  Do every part of this at race pace.  You are trying to nail every run at your most efficient race pace.  Be sure to rest enough between runs that you aren't too tired to maintain this pace throughout the course.

The objective of this workout is to identify your optimum pace.  Most people lose races by going too hard at the start and burning out before the end, a mistake most would never make if they were racing around a track.  The way to identify your ideal pace is to find your fastest run on each third, by doing them separately, and then have each section of your full length lag those ideal times by the same amount.  The first time most people do this workout they find that their top split on the full will be about the same as if they had sprinted through that section, and their bottom split will be down by more than four seconds.  By comparison, I find that I usually lose about a second and a half per section on an ideal run.

Personal Notes:

## Workout: 2 x 8(30" on, 30" off)

Type: Lactic-Tolerance

Protocol: Set an extremely open and easy course. Your objective is to go at a super intense pace, so make the course such that you can really open up. I tend to put an attainment up a drop at the start of the course so that I get the extra incentive of needing to go hard to finish the course.

Intensity: As hard as you can go at that moment in time. That means that you do not pace yourself for 30 seconds and do not pace yourself to do all 16 runs. You will go hard and you will fade. How little or much you fade is your challenge.

This is extremely standard lactic tolerance. Expect to be tired enough to make execution of moves quite difficult. Try focusing on being clean since it is easy to mess up and have dirty runs. Your goal is to keep going hard, and to hold your technique together.

Personal Notes:

## Workout: 3 x 4(40" on, 20"off)

Type: Lactic-Tolerance

Protocol: Set an easy course of maybe four gates or so that is a 40 second loop. I like to put an attainment in this workout, as in all Lactic Tolerance workouts, to inspire me to go even harder. Make sure your course is open and easy so that you can really hammer through it

Intensity: You need to do this workout at your utmost pace. Do not pace yourself even to make it all the way through the 40 seconds. Your runs should start out extremely hard and then fade as little as possible throughout.

This is one of the hardest lactic tolerance workouts that I do. It has actually made me sick on several occasions. I do this at top speed and they should hurt a lot. This, and the full minute lactic tolerance, are the hardest workouts of this type that I know of. I usually do not do this workout within three weeks of a major race since it takes so much out of me. Instead, I substitute easier lactic tolerance workouts into my training plan such as McLoops.

Personal Notes:

## Workout: "Berger Loops", 45' course x 2(4 runs at 40' rest, three runs at 30' rest, three runs at 20' rest)

Type: Lactic-Tolerance

Protocol: This is a hard one to figure out. I named them after Brian "Berger" Homberg who taught me this workout in 1990. Strangely he had no memory of it when we did it together three years later. You never change the course length. The only variable in this workout is the amount of time you rest. You will set a 45 second loop that is an easy race course. Then, you'll do four runs, resting 40 seconds after each run. Without stopping you'll do three more runs where you rest 30 seconds between runs. Still without stopping you'll do three more runs where you only rest 20 seconds. Then stop and take a break before doing it all again. I usually rest for about as long as each set took to do. Either way you'll need at least five minutes between sets.

Intensity: You should paddle very hard for these runs. I usually don't make it an all out effort though since I try and keep my quality up on these runs. Focus on going as hard as you can go and still be precise. Your rest should be just a small paddle around to shake all the toxins out of your blood.

This is a great lactic tolerance workout since you get so much rest at the start. This allows you to comfortably keep your quality quite high until you get near the end and begin to crash. Focus on being concise and crisp with good lines and clean runs throughout. This is a great lactic tolerance workout to do right up till a week and half before the race.

Personal Notes:

## Workout: Broken fulls, 3 x 3(40" on, 20" off)

Type: Lactic Tolerance

Protocol: This workout is can be done on any full length slalom course. I've done these on some of the hardest race courses in the world and you can still maintain some terrific quality throughout the workout. Divide your full-length run into three parts that are about forty seconds long. Start each run at full pace and keep it throughout your piece till you finish your first third. Stop in the eddy for twenty seconds before launching yourself out there for another piece. Do this till the finish line. Your rest between sets can be fairly long, but should be longer than five minutes for sure.

Intensity: Do this workout at a very intense pace. Certainly harder than you'd do a race run at, but not so hard you mess up the gates. Your rest should be complete.

Keep the pace high and the quality good. Remember that you're not only trying to do the physical work, you're also trying to maintain race level quality throughout your run. These make a great physical workout between World Cups or other races where you are on the road and may not have access to a great training site.

Personal Notes:

## Workout: 3 x 3(1' on, 20" off)

Type: Lactic-Tolerance

Protocol:  Set an easy, yet longer course that will be a full minute if you loop back to the start.  Make sure you've got some open water to paddle back up in since you'll need that to really keep your pace up. Simply start and do a one minute loop at full pace. When you finish you'll get twenty seconds to get your act together and start again.  Don't stray far from the start since this is a lot less time than you think it will be.

Intensity:  Extremely intense.  You should not pace yourself at all.  At every moment you should be going harder than you think you possible can.

To me this is one of the hardest workouts that can be done. This is the only workout that we do that I don't enjoy and don't look forward to.  I usually eat a very light breakfast and get these out of the way as soon as I can.  Both this and the 40 on, 20 off lactic tolerance workouts are brutal to your training regime. I usually don't do these within about three weeks of a big race.  I tend to do easier lactic tolerance stuff as I get closer and closer to game day.

Personal Notes:

## Workout:  6(4' on, 6' off)

Type: Lactic Tolerance

Protocol:  Set a race course on pretty good whitewater if you have it.  Your course can either be a loop in which you paddle back to the start, or, with that amount of rest, a semi-loop where you get out and walk up the steep part.  Your runs are all out efforts which last four minutes followed by an unusually long rest of six minutes.

Intensity:  You should go race pace for the on-time. Your rest will end up being a little bit of easy paddling to work off the effort followed by a lot of sitting around waiting for your next start.

These are semi-lactic endurance, but I put them here because they are a great way to get into lactic fitness before a big event.  I usually do this starting at about ten weeks before a big event and tapering them off when I get within three weeks.  They are a great way to put a tremendous amount of work into a run.  They are also a tremendous exercise in keeping your technique together throughout a longer, yet very intense, effort.

Personal Notes:

## Workout: Short Courses, 5 x 5(15"-30" on, 2' off)

Type: Strength

Protocol: This is the most standard of all short course workouts. Set a course that is between fifteen and thirty seconds, of whatever difficulty you would like, and repeat it five times with plenty of rest. Do this same thing for between three and six different courses.

Intensity: Go full speed with complete rest.

This workout can take whatever shape you like. Courses can be fast or slow, hard or easy. Most often you will do this workout with a group of people where it is customary to take turns designing the course. Most people use this workout as the basis for all of their technical work. I like this workout very much, but only use a standard "5 x 5" for about half of my short course work. For the remainder you should try and use more focused and deliberate workouts.

Personal Notes:

## Workout: Broken runs, 4 x 4(30" on, 2"+ rest)

Type: Strength

Protocol: Divide a full-length racecourse up into four parts that are between 20 and 30 seconds long. Do runs down the course where you stop at each break point to rest.

Intensity: You should be going all through the course. Your rest should be long enough that you are fully recovered for your next piece. Rest as long as you'd like between runs.

This is a great way to work on technique in the steeper parts of your course. Most technical workouts, due to laziness, are done in a section of the course that you can easily paddle back up. This workout forces you to walk back to the top and get the benefit of racing through the drops and steeper parts of the course. This is quite often done as a competitive workout with a coach or training partner taking your times. Some variations include adding up all of your times and comparing that to a full length run, or else simply racing each other based on a run that is timed and scored and added together. These workouts are often more useful than simple brokens since they force you to have a full quality run instead of one good piece out of five on each section.

Personal Notes:

### Workout:  Impossible moves shorts, 5 x 5(15"-30" on, 2' off)

Type:  Strength

Protocol:  This is my favorite workout to do.  The idea is to set five courses that are beyond the realm of possibility.  If you do this with some extremely keen training partners, this workout can become absolutely obscene.  The moves should require big pivots, head ducks, and lots of scrambling.  Do a simple five by five with these difficult courses

Intensity:  Go full speed with complete rest.

   This is a fantastic workout to use to learn boat control, edging, and scrambling.  It is fun, competitive, and you will get lots of tries at each different course.  The thing to keep in mind is that at any World Cup race, no matter how unrealistic a certain move is, somebody two strokes every up and pegs every offset.  I say do this workout every single chance you get, and be that person.

Personal Notes:

### Workout:  World Cup Shorts, 5 x 5(15"-30" on, 2'+ off)

Type:  Strength

Protocol:  This workout requires a competitive training partner.  Set a course of about race difficulty.  Take one practice run per course before doing two runs that are timed, scored and recorded.  Do this for five different courses (the World Cup is getting longer now, so you may need to do more courses) making sure to take turns designing the course.  The winner for each course, regardless of lead, gets a single point.  Second place will get two points and on up to your last place guy.  The winner of the workout is the one who has the least amount of points at the end.

Intensity:  Go full speed with complete rest.

   World Cup shorts are one of the most competitive workouts you can do.  I like to do these leading into the season since I believe that they make you a tough competitor.  Be sure to keep track of touches in this workout since half the point of doing this is to be competing in a race-like environment.

Personal Notes:

## Workout: Single Shorts, 10 x (20"-30" on, long rest)

Type: Strength

Protocol: Set a difficult course on race difficulty white-water. The course should be a difficult move that would be at or above the level of difficulty you are training to race on. Do a race preparation for this move and then a single run. Evaluate your performance before designing an entirely new move and doing the same thing. Do this for ten courses

Intensity: Go full speed with complete rest.

This workout is all about preparation and it is a workout that is used to test and work on your race performance. The idea behind it is to see whether or not you can fully prepare for a move at or near the extreme end of your ability and then execute that move successfully on your first try. Remember that with combined runs you must be able to perfectly execute race runs every single time! Be sure that, if the weather is cold, you dress warmly enough to be out in the wet and cold without working very much since this workout requires very little effort and a lot of standing around.

A note to the coaches: I often do this workout in training camps with video. Without informing any of the participants of my intentions I let them prepare for a single run, but then put them aside, out of view of the course, before they start. Once back there I ask them to tell the video their race plan and then film their run. I use one video cassette per athlete so that you see their race plan immediately before you see their execution. I have very rarely seen an athlete who was fully prepared to start a race run.

Personal Notes:

## Workout: Short Courses, 5 x 5(15"-30" on, 2' off)

Type: Strength

Protocol: Do a standard short course workout with a large group. Set courses that are between fifteen and thirty seconds, of whatever difficulty you would like. Now, divide the people in your workout into two equally sized groups of equal ability. If there are an odd number of people, then stick the coach in to even up the sides. Take turns setting courses between the teams. You can use any system of scoring that you like in order to decide which team beats the other on each course. I like to actually pair competitors up against each other and give points to whichever of the two manages to be the best over two runs combined. You could also add up the times for the entire team over two runs.

Intensity: Go full speed with complete rest.

Team shorts are a fantastic workout for team spirit and competition. They tend to be fierce, fun, and loud, all of which are fantastic attributes for a training session. Another fun variation is to actually do a single course as a team run. This is great practice for team racing and adds a lot of variety to a workout.

Personal Notes:

### Workout:  Scored Shorts, 5 x 5(15"-30" on, 2' off)

Type:  Strength

Protocol:  This is really a standard short course workout.  Set a course that is between fifteen and thirty
seconds, of whatever difficulty you would like, and
repeat it five times with plenty of rest.  Do this
same thing for between three and six different
courses.  Instead of timing each run have your training partners score your run on a scale of one to
four.  Your score should be based solely on execution of the moves, not on time or effort.  Try and
focus on being smooth, on letting the boat glide,
and on being precise and crisp.

Intensity:  Go near race pace with complete rest.

This is one of the few competitive workouts that you
will do without being timed.  Your score is a measure
of your finesse and form.  I like this workout because
the priority is on perfection rather than brute strength
and time.  It is also a good workout to do with paddlers of similar ability, but different speeds, such as
people from other classes.

Personal Notes:

### Workout:  Funnel Sprints, 2 x 4(30" on, 30" off, 30" on) 2 x 6(10"on, 50"off)

Type:  Strength

Protocol:  Make a funnel out of the top of a two-liter
bottle of soda.  I make the funnel by cutting the
bottle in half and taking the lid off the top.  I then
make a simple halter out of three cords tied around
the open mouth of the half-bottle.  Tie this to your
boat with about 6 feet of cord (enough that you can
take the funnel out and put it in your lap when you
rest).  Do the thirty-second sprints by taking doing
your ultimately powerful stroke, but then pausing
for a slow recovery before doing the same on the
other side.  This is not a workout where you want
to run your pulse up very high.  Your focus should
be to make each single stroke a maximal effort
without racing your pulse too high.  If you need to
wear a pulse-rate-monitor, don't let your pulse go
much above an End 1 pace.

For the ten-second pieces you should be going all
out.  You want to make these a hard fast effort with
complete and well-executed strokes.  Do not sacrifice
technique by rushing your strokes too much.

Intensity:  Go full speed with complete rest.

The interesting thing about this workout is that it is
actually fantastic for your stroke technique!  You would
think that the added load would cause your stroke to
waver and flutter, but instead you'll find yourself much
more in control of each effort.  The drag should slow
down your stroke but still allow you to apply a maximal
effort, similar to when you sprint.  This will let you pick
apart each stroke under full power!  This is a fantastic
way to evaluate your stroke.

Personal Notes:

## Workout: Consistency Loop Technique

Type: Lactic/Technique

Protocol: Set a two or three gate course that empha-
sizes basic technique. The most common version of
this course would be two gates on the same wire
done as a continuous loop of double upstreams (a
figure eight). Do the course once at race pace to
get a single run target time. Now add between ten
and twenty percent to this time and set this as your
lower limit. Your challenge now is to loop this
course for as long as possible without touching the
poles or falling below your lower limit. Have a
coach time each single loop. Focus on consistent
well-executed technique and crisp lines.

Intensity: Within twenty percent of race pace. Take
longer full rests between sets.

This workout is a great hybrid of technical and physical work. Athletes should focus on consistently repeat-
ing perfect runs through a simple course despite
fatigue and competitive pressure. This can also be a
great competitive workout between athletes of vastly
different speeds and abilities. Simply see who can stay
within their limits the longest, everyone's time should
be set relative to their own personal ability.
I have also seen this workout done in teams to add
the challenge of another, albeit moving, obstacle to
your concentration. Paddlers then must not only execute the course consistently, but also weave consistently with their competitors.

Personal Notes:

## Workout: Specific Technique

Type: Strength. /Technique

Protocol: Set a specific workout goal before you even
get on the water and make this the focus of your
workout. Then set courses that isolate and work
this specific objective throughout the workout. I try
and make the courses as short as I possibly can and
still focus on the objective at hand. For upstreams
in the current this can make the course one single
gate long. For offsets the courses can be as long as
a continuous half-length.

Intensity: It should vary depending on the objective of
the workout. Intensities could be as easy as your
easiest pace or as intense as your most difficult.

This workout is really the putty with which you will
shape your abilities. I have seen a million workouts
where athletes get on the water and ask a coach or a
training partner what they want to work on. Do not let
yourself become one of the sheep-like masses! Decide
what you need to work on and focus yourself so that
your workouts exactly isolate that one skill!

Personal Notes:

### Workout: Teacher Technique

Type: Strength/Technique

Protocol: This was a great workout for me in times when I had a fantastic training group but did not have a coach. Rather than having a coach shape, schedule and fit our workouts to our technical priorities we did it ourselves. Each week one member of the training group was in charge of both deciding what the technical objective for this workout would be and deciding how and where we would work these skills. This made for a fantastic variety in what we worked as well as a very thorough approach to covering a multitude of different skills.

Intensity: This should vary according to priority.

This is a great way to work technique in a group environment. Training groups tend to develop a leader who will most likely set a very homogenous training routine. It is better to get everyone involved in course design and technical analysis. It is also a way to insure that you have a huge variety in your training.

Personal Notes:

### Workout: Easy to Hard Technique

Type: Strength/Technique

Protocol: Set a relatively easy gate combination that is the length of a short course (15" to 30" long). Repeat runs on this course until you feel you are having perfect runs. Once mastered, move the gates on this same course into more difficult positions and repeat. Take this to the extreme where you are working an impossibly hard version of your original course. Try and maintain the good form you practiced at the start throughout this workout.

Intensity: Race Pace.

This is a particularly good way to work good offset technique in a focused workout. Each run is an attainable extension of the course you managed with perfect technique minutes before. You will find that you can quickly run through extremely hard courses while still keeping extremely good technique.

Personal Notes:

## Workout: Big Drop Technique

Type: Strength/Technique

Protocol: Set hard moves in whitewater that you cannot paddle back up. Carry back up to repeat courses as many times as it takes to get them consistently right. Once mastered, change the course and begin again. This workout can take some time because you will spend more time walking back up than you will paddling down the river. Go ahead and spend a couple hours getting this workout done right.

Intensity: Race Pace.

This can be the workout that separates the dedicated from the merely involved. Especially on cold, wet and miserable days. It is often quite easy to set courses below the big drops and bang in run after run while easily paddling back to the top for the next repetition. However, it is the athlete who practices hard moves in the drops and in the big water that will dominate the races. Take the time to carry back up and practice racing the way you will see it in the races.

Personal Notes:

## Workout: Important Stroke Technique

Type: Strength/Technique

Protocol: This workout is quite similar to a five by five workout in technique. Set five short courses that are between 15 and 30 seconds in length. Do as many runs per course as you would like, all of them at full speed. The catch is this, that you have to do less strokes on every run. Eventually you will be gliding for the larger part of your run and taking strokes only when it is absolutely crucial. This should identify which strokes are key, and when.

Intensity: Race pace or higher.

Slalom involves a bunch of scrambling to get in position for a few key strokes. Most super hard moves depend on one well-timed and well-executed stroke. You can use this workout to identify and practice these crux maneuvers.

Personal Notes:

## Workout: Technique Singles

Type: Strength/Technique

Protocol: Set difficult short courses on difficult white-water. These courses should mimic the harder moves on a racecourse. Now go through your entire race preparation as if the consequences of your actions were going to affect your most important race. Decide whether you will take a risk or be cautious, decide whether you will go faster or slower, decide everything as if this were the Olympics and you had one single shot to get it right. When you are ready, take that single shot and evaluate your performance. Change the course and do this again.

Intensity: Race Pace

This is the best workout there is for linking up your self-perceptions with your actual ability. When you are good at this workout you should have a fairly accurate idea about your chances on any course anywhere. This is also a great workout to evaluate whether you are visualizing an accurate prediction of what your eventual race run will be.

Coaches Note: I also do this workout at training camps as an introduction to race preparation. I usually bring a videotape for each athlete involved in the workout. I then set a short course and ask the athletes to start when they are ready. Usually they all head directly to the start. I then pull them aside, out of sight of the course, and have them recite their race plan, which I record on their personal videotape. I then video their runs directly after their commentary. This makes a shocking comparison between what they had planned, planned with little preparation, and what they eventually did out on the slalom course.

Personal Notes:

## Workout: Technique, Slow to Fast Shorts

Type: Strength/Technique

Protocol: Set courses that are of any difficulty and between 15 and 30 seconds long. Do six runs on the course, steadily increasing your pace on each run. You should start at a pace just above normal warm-up pace and finish at a fanatically fast rate. Take times on each run to try and find an ideal race pace. It is important that you try and maintain good technique throughout your runs so that you can identify your ideal pace at which you can execute a perfect run.

Intensity: Varying

This workout is good for people who are having trouble with either going too hard, or not hard enough. In general I find that I do better with runs that are at or near the pace I find myself at on my fourth run. A coach is a fantastic tool in this workout because they have the perspective of seeing the athlete's run in the third person. This gives them an absolute view of where the athlete is faster or slower and more or less frantic. I aim for smooth, crisp, and precise technique.

Personal Notes:

## Workout: Whitewater Moves Technique

Type: Strength/Technique

Protocol: Go out on any whitewater river that has well defined waves and holes and set courses that use these features for mock upstreams, ferries, and S-turns. Repeat these courses until you feel that you are using the water to the greatest advantage possible. Ignore your mock course in favor of unlocking the secrets of using the water.

Intensity: Pace should vary.

Every single facet of your run should have been isolated and worked by the time you start your race run this year. Often though it is the obvious skills, the whitewater skills, that are ignored in favor of gate work. Take the time to learn to use a wave to shoot across a river, to learn to bank off of a hole without losing your balance, to learn all the nuances of using the river instead of muscling your way down the course. Often these courses are shorter than ten-seconds in the interest of working on crossing a single wave or hole. Remember to focus your workout on the objective you think is most important!

Personal Notes:

## Workout: C-1 Shorts Technique

Type: Strength/Technique

Protocol: Do a typical five by five workout with courses between 15 and 30 seconds long. Do your first run normally but then do your next two runs as a C-1 on alternate sides. You should find that in each combination paddling on one side works much better than the other. Use this analysis to plan your subsequent two runs by identifying which strokes, on which sides, are key to a successful run. Repeat this throughout your workout

Intensity: Race Pace.

This is a good way to identify key strokes and to practice them. It is also a great workout for edge and blade control. You will develop an innate sense of your edges and paddle by doing this. You'll also flip, crash and burn throughout the workout. Treat it as a learning experience. Another variation is to do runs on these same courses backwards to emphasize to further emphasize the work on your boat and edge control. Bill Endicott has claimed that five-time World Champion Richard Fox could do a fair version of a run while going backwards and only paddling as a C-1 limited to cross-bow strokes. It could be Fox had trouble filling up his spare time.

Personal Notes:

## About the Author:

Scott Shipley is a three-time Olympian and three-time World Cup Champion. He is known for a consistent and flowing paddling style which propelled him to the medal stand at the World Championships and World Cup for eight-consecutive years-winning medals at eighty percent of the World Cups in which he competed. Shipley began his paddling career in the Pacific Northwest and, in the twenty-four years that he raced competitively, has competed in over thirty countries as a member of the U.S. National team.

Photo by Chris Smith.